Living On/To Survive
Epidemic Writings

Also by the Author

Posthumously: For Jacques Derrida
HB 978-1-84519-432-1   £45.00 / $62.50
PB 978-1-84519-778-0   £22.50 / $34.95

Encounters: Gérard Titus-Carmel, Jean-Luc Nancy, Claire Denis
HB 978-1-84519-663-9   £45.00 / $60.00
PB 978-1-84519-715-5   £27.50 / $39.95

On Contemporaneity: The Concept and its Times
PB 978-1-84519-991-3   £29.95 / $39.95

On Contemporaneity, after Agamben: Art in the time that remains . . .
PB 978-1-84519-992-0   £29.95 / $39.95
Due November 2022

Living On/To Survive
Epidemic Writings

ZSUZSA BAROSS

ACADEMIC
PRESS
Brighton • Chicago • Toronto

Copyright © Zsuzsa Baross 2022.

The right of Zsuzsa Baross to be identified as Author of this work has been asserted in accordance with the Copyright, Designs and Patents Act 1988.

2 4 6 8 10 9 7 5 3 1

First published in Great Britain in 2022 by
SUSSEX ACADEMIC PRESS
PO Box 139, Eastbourne BN24 9BP

Distributed in North America by
SUSSEX ACADEMIC PRESS
Independent Publishers Group
814 N. Franklin Street
Chicago, IL 60610

All rights reserved. Except for the quotation of short passages for the purposes of criticism and review, no part of this publication may be reproduced, stored in a retrieval system, or transmitted, in any form or by any means, electronic, mechanical, photocopying, recording or otherwise, without the prior permission of the publisher.

British Library Cataloguing in Publication Data
A CIP catalogue record for this book is available from the British Library.

Library of Congress Cataloging-in-Publication Data
To be applied For.

Paperback ISBN 978-1-78976-115-3

Typeset and designed by Sussex Academic Press, Brighton & Eastbourne.

Contents

Preface   vi

Agamben, the Virus, and the Biopolitical: A Riposte   1

Philosophy in the Time of the Epidemic: Two Transcripts   18

On the Absence of the World, One More Time;   30
Or, Finding the World, Again

Sur-vie   91

Appendix: JLN   109
1. For Jean-Luc Nancy, Posthumously   110
2. The Last Interview   117
3. JLN's Library (Fragment)   121

Preface

Those familiar with the work of Jacques Derrida will recognize the double term in the book's title as variations in translation of Derrida's untimely essay "Survivre." "To survive"—in the infinitive mood and in this indefinite form that sets no limit to number, person, or time—is at once the theme and the undercurrent that runs through the diverse texts gathered together in the volume. The writings date from the time of the pandemic—from its different times and mutating phases—still on course as I am writing this Preface here. Placed in chronological order, their critical reflection on the ominous sense of this "novel" virus and crisis also registers the progressive evolution and complication of this new sense that a critical threshold, perhaps the last, may have been crossed. "To survive," however, for such is our exceptional situation, also animates the act of writing, of turning to writing. In the profound crisis of our existence, or as in Agamben's recent title, *When the House is Burning (Quando la casa bracia)*, *sur-vie* becomes an affair, if not the affair of writing. Paradoxically, it alone holds out, as possible, the promise of a survival that is more than bare life. Derrida termed it "sur-vie," in the English translation of his long essay, "living on."

With one exception, each text was prepared for an occasion. The first is contemporaneous with the immediate outbreak of the epidemic and with Agamben's provocative dismissal of it as a "health" emergency. The "Two Transcripts" are of video interventions that appeared on Jérôme Lèbre's YouTube channel "Philosopher en temps d'épidémie"—one of several platforms to immediately call for critical discourse to intervene in the

Preface

crisis. A third intervention, completing the triptych, was recorded in French but is yet be published. Here an extended and substantially developed version responds to the (un)timeliness of Derrida's early essay "Survivre." At the center of the volume, anchoring the collection, is the text that was also the most difficult to write "On the Absence of the World . . ." in the midst of the pandemic. It returns to my earlier discussion (in *On Contemporaneity, after Agamben*) to Derrida's interventions in / translations of Paul Celan's today prophetic verse "The world is gone." The essay thus may be read as a belated postscript to this first volume—which appeared in early 2020 but was completed just before the epidemic—and / or as a premature preface that prepares the ground for the next volume, yet to be written on *Art in the Time That Remains*.

The three short texts in "Appendix: JLN" are staggered responses to the recent death of Jean-Luc Nancy, the news of which arrived after the texts planned for the volume had been completed. While the news of this *disparition* was not entirely unexpected, its subterranean effects continue to reverberate even today, differently / differingly with the passage of time. The writing in the Appendix registers some of these tremors in three micro-variations on the theme announced by the book's title: *living on / to survive.*

Agamben, the Virus, and the Biopolitical: A Riposte

Our society no longer believes in anything but bare life. It is obvious that Italians are disposed to sacrifice practically everything—the normal conditions of life, social relationships, work, even friendships, affections and religious and political convictions—to the danger of getting sick. Bare life—and the danger of losing it—is not something that unites people, but blinds and separates them. (Agamben, "Clarifications," 17/03/2020)[1]

The mistake, or shall I say after Deleuze, the *bêtise*, of Agamben's response to the new coronavirus ("the invention of an epidemic"[2]) is not that it mistakes the pathogen for a "normal" flu, an infection whose victims are small in number and, for the most part, with light or moderate symptoms (even though by late February when the first provocative piece appeared,[3] the

---

This essay first appeared in the *European Journal of Psychoanalysis*, May 12, 2020; it was subsequently republished in paper form in *Coronavirus, Psychoanalysis and Philosophy*, eds. Fernando Castrillon and Thomas Marchevsky, London: Routledge, 2021.

I am writing this at the beginning of April 2020, only a few short weeks after Agamben's first intervention, during which period the virus has escaped definitions, evaded defensive measures, outpaced projections, predictions, prognoses . . . This viral inventiveness, however, is only one reason why I will not engage Agamben regarding the nature of the virus nor predicate on it the discussion here.

scale of the devastation in Wuhan and elsewhere was evident, whether or not it constituted an "event" [that Agamben invites us to reread François Brune's *Ces évènements qui n'existent pas* implies that the answer to this question should be negative]; besides the question of competence, the category "normal" has a questionable place in virology, as the history of epidemics, as the devastation of the natives of the Americas attest. Viruses "normalize" or/and get "normalized.")

But Agamben, as he will remind his critics in a later interview,[4] is not an epidemiologist or virologist; he does not intervene in the question in the capacity of a specialist in infectious diseases. The error (this time neither mistake nor *bêtise*) concerns not the nature of the virus itself (which is Nancy's argument) but lies at the very heart of his philosophical project and its application/invocation of the (old) concept of the biopolitical (and the state of exception as its purest form) with regard to the time of the day, today: the time of the "geocide" (Michel Deguy), the climate "collapse," the generalized catastrophe (collapse of coordinates) . . . The flaw in the argument that the fear of the manufactured epidemic is (put) in the service of the political (governments) and responds to the real need for a collective panic—for which the "epidemic is an ideal pretext"—is not that it underestimates the force or potency of the epidemic for (biological, economic, social, cultural) devastation (which it does); nor does it lie in reading the aggressive governmental responses to the epidemic as essentially and fundamentally "biopolitical"; rather, it lies in failing to grasp these responses as manifestations and symptoms of a radical mutation in the field: the inversion of the *order* of the articulation *bio/political*, the *detournement* and reversal of the direction of forces that traverse the nexus which inexorably, irrevocably, and today without mercy, binds "bios" (organic and inorganic life) to the political.

A Riposte

The "biopolitical"

As we know, Agamben's re-appropriation of Foucault's concept (in *Homo Sacer*) turns the biopolitical into an axiomatic "thesis": the political (of the West) is always already biopolitical, is constituted as such, as the exclusion (fabrication) of "bare life" at the point of its origin (Aristotle, the Greeks). I leave aside here my reservation regarding this initial founding gesture and recall only that Hannah Arendt's reading (in *The Human Condition*) of the same history generates a different structure and narrative of the origin. It assigns the creation of the political—the founding distinction/division (*oikos/polis*; *zoe/bios*)—to the performative work of the Law that belongs to neither domain. The Law (or the Wall, the physical manifestation of the nomos) orders the city it constitutes into two distinct spaces it itself separates: *oikos*, or the private space of "privation" (production/reproduction // need and necessity // birth and death . . .), and *polis*, or the public space of visibility, exposure, action. True, the *polis* excludes *zoe* from its domain: the "metabolism of life" is hidden from view on the other side of the Wall by the Wall. But the Wall, this early precursor of "separation," unlike the contemporary variety that creates enclaves, only separates, sorts out, makes a categorical distinction; the Greek citizen, the citizen-body, crosses over the Wall daily and is the habitant of both domains. In other words, the *polis* excludes, but does not capture, hold captive what it excludes. The structure, *oikos/polis*, in this Arendtian rendition, is irreducibly heterogeneous to the "inclusive exclusion" yet to come in the future, whose "paradigm is the camp," which in turn is the "nomos of the modern" (see paragraphs 5 and 7 of *Homo Sacer*).

One need not embrace Arendt's narrative reconstruction of the origin to see the slippage (perhaps even sleight of hand) in Agamben regarding Foucault's biopolitical. The "always already" smooths over, flattens out, the disruptive gesture of Foucault's genealogy, which cuts into the flow of history, inserting into it the discontinuity of a heterogenizing mutation; namely, a new political or governmentality that, unlike the sovereign power it replaces, takes charge of life. In Agamben's revision, the Foucauldian genealogy of heterogeneous formations is contracted, its discontinuity replaced by a long and continuous biopolitical history and "development" (I use his term with caution as a shorthand), which, while filled with repetitions, resemblances, precursors, forgotten originals, and returns, is still, in the last instance, always the biopolitical fabrication of bare life. In its purest, that is, most reductive form, the biopolitical becomes the state of exception—the most reductive form and absolute limit case with regard to both life and, paradoxically, the political itself, for absolute power over absolutely reduced life is achieved at the cost of the Law rendering itself inoperative, by law. "It encompasses living beings by means of its own [lawful] suspension" (*State of Exception*, 3).

We can see how the emergencies recently declared all over the world would lead or permit Agamben to recognize in them the classical *form* of the state of exception, now normalized:

> What is once again manifest is the tendency to use a state of exception as a normal paradigm for government. The legislative decree immediately approved by the government "for hygiene and public safety reasons" actually produces an authentic militarization "of the municipalities and areas with the presence of at least one person who tests positive and for whom the source of transmission is unknown, or in which there is at least one case that is not ascribable to a person who recently returned from an area already affected by the virus". Such a vague and undetermined definition will make it possible to rapidly extend the state of exception to all regions, as it's almost impossible that other such cases will not appear elsewhere. Let's consider the serious limitations of freedom the decree contains: a) a prohibition against any individuals leaving the affected municipality or area; b) a prohibition

A Riposte

against anyone from outside accessing the affected municipality or area; c) the suspension of events or initiatives of any nature and of any form of gatherings in public or private places, including those of a cultural, recreational, sporting and religious nature, including enclosed spaces if they are open to the public; d) the closure of kindergartens, childcare services and schools of all levels, as well as the attendance of school, higher education activities and professional courses, except for distance learning; e) the closure to the public of museums and other cultural institutions and spaces as listed in article 101 of the code of cultural and landscape heritage, pursuant to Legislative Decree 22 January 2004, no. 42. All regulations on free access to those institutions and spaces are also suspended; f) suspension of all educational trips both in Italy and abroad; g) suspension of all public examination procedures and all activities of public offices, without prejudice to the provision of essential and public utility services; h) the enforcement of quarantine measures and active surveillance of individuals who have had close contacts with confirmed cases of infection. ("The Invention of an Epidemic")

Whether at the point of its origin or, for Agamben, in its purest state, the state of exception, or again, in its latest variety of bio-economico-political order—power always flows from the political in the direction of life: toward its regulation, control, dressage, confinement; its manipulation, exploitation, putting it to work (see insulin production), turning it to a weapon (biological warfare); or, as power becomes ever more creative, it moves towards recombination (DNA), transplantation, hybridization, manufacture . . . and, in the last instance, not in terms of chronology, the fabrication of life as bare life . . .

The state of exception therefore is also exceptional in this regard: it targets to control the whole of life.

As structure, perhaps, but certainly as (empty) *form*, the state of exception would appear to cover—as a lid covers what falls under it—the multiple ever more draconian, ever more restrictive regulations recently enacted: distancing, spacing, quarantine, confinement, self-isolation, and, most recently, the tracking of movements and contacts of bodies—citizen bodies.

And yet, something escapes. First, the virus escapes. Literally.[5] From the rainforest of the Democratic Republic of the Congo, from the wild (wild life: bat, pangolin—a rare anteater) in Wuhan, a life form escapes, an RNA sequence that is not even properly alive. It leaps over the barrier between species, escapes its confinement to "nature," its assigned proper (own) territory. Following, opportunistically exploiting the routes and pathways of globalization—that other aggressive, indiscriminate invader—it itself globalizes, but englobes not the globe or the earth, but the World.[6] In Jean-Luc Nancy's terminology: space(s) where sense circulates. In Deleuze's language, it deterritorializes from "nature," the "wild" (or the bio-lab), and simultaneously reterritorializes (there is no deterritorialization without reterritorialization) the "socio-political domain"; it leaps over to the other side of the Wall of separation that long ago constituted its territory by confining it on the inside. In other words, the direction of invasion, intervention, penetration—that is, of forces passing though the nexus—gets reversed: now they flow from the direction of life; the *sense* (in every sense of this word) of the bio-political gets inverted as it is the political body/the body of the political that is invaded, attacked. The tissue of connections that make and remake this body is torn apart, in self-defense; the biological, living citizen-body is forced to retreat from public spaces, to take refuge in the space of privation, the *oikos*, leaving the virus to circulate in the public space, more or less freely. (And not just the virus: as we learnt recently, wild animals, foxes, coyotes, have been returning to the streets of the city. In South Africa, a pride of

A Riposte

lions has been photographed sleeping lazily on an empty highway.) The state of exception (if this term still applies) in the case of this "novel" virus is not the exercise of power over life as bare life, but, on the contrary, an extreme (exceptional) self-defensive measure and immune reaction by the political body to an invading life form that is not even properly alive.

The bio-political: we have been so certain, so confident of our control over our own "invention" (as Agamben understands this term, as a political construction) "nature," as distinct and separate, a domain apart, that our language left out the hyphen that would mark the conjunction, designating the place of articulation where forces cross over, and which is also the weakest point in the construction, opening up the *concept* to deconstruction, on the one hand, and the political, the life and the only life our societies have known for some time, to a potentially total destruction, on the other. The notion (again Agamben's) that the "contagion" would be an invention of the political is thus a fantasy that belongs to this same old biopolitical order, without a hyphen, whose order (ordering of the relation) has been overturned, whose forces (first "containment," then "mitigation") have been, to stay with the war metaphors so popular nowadays, de-routed and, so far, defeated. Not just by the newly discovered, infinitely inventive virus, but by the far more massive and irreversible contagion that will not go away when "all this ends," and has been on course for some time: the climate catastrophe, collapse or geocide, which is the terrain on which this epidemic unfolds, their common "transmitter" being, as we well know, globalization.

The bio-political response to the contagion, a state of exception, is thus a defensive immune reaction, or more precisely, a reaction of auto-immunity (in Derrida's precise definition of this term) that turns against the very body it is designed to defend. It acts into, destroys the connective tissue of the political body: it interrupts the flow of communication, closes border crossings, isolates, prohibits contact, confines, excludes, isolates; it punctuates public spaces by opening up gaps, inserting intervals; it empties cinemas and theaters, turns the grand boulevards of great cities into deserts, commands a distance large enough between bodies to prevent con-tact even by the air exhaled. (In its mechanism of auto-defense, the political thus mimics the living body, whose excessive immune reaction to the virus destroys the body itself: floods the lungs and, depriving it of oxygen, brings about its total organ failure.)

"Bare life" vs. "A life"

A personal digression is perhaps permissible at the time of this pandemic: for days the phrase or syntagma "born to life" has been circulating in my head. I thought it was in reference to "bare life." Naked or nude? I've asked myself. Which is the more appropriate term? And what is the difference? One is born nude but certainly not naked; one is born into a web of relations, to a language, that is, to a world, where sense circulates and which *makes* sense (in every sense), however senseless this world may appear. At least, this is how Hannah Arendt understood nativity—born to a language, to a World. Across the distance of their different philosophies, these notions also correspond with Benjamin's condition of what is "man," at least in one reading of his inherently, incurably enigmatic "Critique of Violence": "existence, that is 'life' is irreducible to the total condition that is 'man'"; and in an even stronger formulation: "man cannot at any price coincide with the mere life in him" (*Selected Writings, Vol. 1*, 251). By consequence, naked or bare life, the *blosse Leben* of Benjamin that Agamben often cites, is secondary; it cannot be the original, the first condition. On the contrary, it comes after, is something extracted from life itself and not the result of a violent separation or dispossession of acquired attributes and qualifications. In other words, bare

A Riposte

life is the product of an operation and, as such, not a thing. It is relational, possible only within a structure imposed in/by/through a political relation.

I soon realize that the syntagma's origin is Aristotle, or rather Agamben's reading of Aristotle's *Politics*: "man is born with regard to life but exist[(s)] essentially with regard to good life." Aristotle's categorical distinction is in fact the kernel of Agamben's "biopolitical" thesis: the original political relation is the exclusion of existence as bare life. It also allows for a different reading of Benjamin's enigma, one that forces the ambivalence mentioned above in the other direction—that of a moral contempt for the ignominy (Benjamin's term) of a life that would voluntarily choose bare life, clinging onto existence at all cost, to nothing but the bare life (in life). In other words, a contempt for the Italians in their willingness to surrender every political right, even sociality (family, friendship, funerals), to escape from the sickness of the virus. (This same moral contempt may also explain why, many decades ago, Agamben advised Jean-Luc Nancy not have the heart transplant that saved his life.) For confirmation, Agamben again cites Aristotle: "if there is no great difficulty as to the way of life [*kata ton bion*], clearly most men will tolerate much suffering and hold onto life (*zoe*) as if it were a kind of serenity [*euemereia*, beautiful day] and a natural sweetness" (*Homo Sacer*, 2).

Something, however, remains unaccounted for: the "as if" of Aristotle. As if we could or should read it as casting doubt upon the reality of the "beautiful day" and natural sweetness, or upon what Glenn Gould characterized in Bach's method of composition—its endless detours, delays, and refusal to reach the end—as what matters (in music): the "joyous essence of being."

What if we read Aristotle's "as if" otherwise? Pointing to the founding gesture of the *concept* itself whose own division of the life-world *bios/zoe* is founded on the (non-inclusive) exclusion of a remainder: something of life, not bare life but the "beautiful day," which is the remainder of the conceptional division that neither register, neither *bios* (qualified life) nor *zoe* (bare life), can accommodate.

Today, more than ever it seems, we need to return to this unaccounted-for remainder; especially today, at the time of this epidemic, we need to recuperate it from its exile underground, as we—not just the Italians but the whole world—tremble in the face of a globalizing threat to life in each and every one of us.

In Foucault's original construction (invention), the biopolitical opens a path in another possible direction, leading away from drawing any direct or indirect line between the agonizing body of the coronavirus patient in the hospital bed and the death camp ("the nomos of the modern political"). This new paradigm of governmentality takes charge of life, even if only life and nothing but biological life. No matter how reductive a concept of life its bios may be, unlike existence—static, as it were, lifeless—bio is "vital," the terrain of dynamic articulations, the encounter of forces/intensities/sensations . . . In the original construction, the concept cuts up things in the world differently; its new political invests itself in life, manages living, the biological existence of the living, whose powers it enhances, whose force and capacities it amplifies and augments, whose life span it prolongs (see Michel Serres' celebrations of the biopolitical advances made in the last century: the eradication of diseases, the reduction of poverty and hunger, the extension of life expectancy, etc., across the world). For this reason, the biopolitical is embarrassed in the face of death as evidence or proof of its failure. (Hence one more reason for the embarrassment at the rising number of infections and the death toll. Trump lies about it, the Russians, the Iranians and, at the outbreak, the Chinese try to hide it.)

It is perhaps safe to say that the political response to the pandemic has been biopolitical in Foucault's classical definition of the concept: a practice of governmentality that takes charge of the ensemble of the living, in this case, of the

A Riposte

mechanics of life as concerns the health, hygiene, survival, and death of a *population*. ("Flattening the curve" is exemplary in this regard: it is concerned with the survival *rate* of the population, and hence with "herd immunity," the spread and incidence of the infection over time, and not with the life of the individual (saving lives)). But it would be an error to deduce from this that the reactive agent itself is the same old biopolitical. In the age of mondialization—when "population" is fluid, constantly de- and re-constituted at different geographic locations by a mobile and migrant capital in search of the lowest cost—governmental practices have long renounced the one form of biopower; namely, the fostering of life, and aggressively maintained instead only the other component, withdrawing from life to the point of death. Rather than a continued extension/expansion of biopolitics, the current emergency measures are reactivations of old forms. The virus forces governments to rediscover the "population" they abandoned long ago; or rather, it itself reconstitutes or recomposes, with great force, the masses of disparate, atomized bodies living in cities, regions, and states into the living body of a collective collectively exposed, infected and infectious, contaminated and contaminating . . . [7] Just as it exposes the impower of the digital, the virtual, the artificial, the gig economy, the forces of immaterialization, derivatives, bitcoin, the financial industry . . . and the power of life and of the material real (masks, ventilators, protective clothing, medicines; the daily food supply, life-saving medicines, even toilet paper). Just as it exposes the extraordinary and extraordinarily unexploited power of the living *body* of the most downtrodden, the "essential" labor of migrants and minorities; of the truck driver, the janitor, the garbage collector, the bus driver, the mailman, the cashier, the distributor, the grocery clerk, the fireman, the delivery man; of orderlies and caregivers in old-age homes, workers in meat processing plants, seasonal agricultural laborers, and by extension, those hands responsible for milking cows, feeding pigs, gathering eggs, baking breads, picking fruits . . .

If it is not (necessarily/immediately) in the hospital bed, in the intubated body hooked up to a ventilator, that we find bare life today, then where is it? What region of this globalized political is its proper habitat? Has it vanished from the theater of the political? In fact, it is everywhere (different geological planes/plates of the political co-exist, are contiguous, in the same chronological time). It is, for example, the body bobbing in the Mediterranean Sea, clinging onto the side of a packed inflatable; it is the body "kettled" behind barbed-wire fencing of camps on all sides at both edges of Europe; it is caged into the enclave outside Idlib, Syria, and crowded onto a sliver of dry land between two bodies of filthy water on the border between Bangladesh and Myanmar . . .

The question is then how to rescue what necessarily falls in between, exists in the gap between life's nakedness and its full qualification (person, personality, the singularity of its quality), between political life and bare life? How to rescue by way of a concept or concepts the sweetness Aristotle spoke of, and rescue it as irreducible to fear (of death), to instinct (of survival), clinging onto life at any cost (which earns Agamben's contempt and Benjamin's characterization as ignoble)? How to rescue that element or dimension—but what is the right word here? Is it not sense?—the *sense* (in every sense of this word) of life, whose "non-existence would be something more terrible" (says Benjamin) than any "attained" condition of man?

The body clinging onto the side of an overcrowded inflatable, the body that makes one last effort to cross the desert, is bare life: standing in a relation, even in it its absolute solitude and abandonment. It is a creation, a product manufactured by the machinery of a political that expelled it precisely from the world into which it was born. In fact, from the World itself. Outside the law but held by the law outside the World. On the other hand, what *Aquarius* and the other rescue ships are searching for

A Riposte

in the open sea, what the volunteers combing the desert of Texas for refugees hope to save, is a third category of living existence. Deleuze gave it the simple name: *a* life.

> No one has described better what a life is than Charles Dickens ... A disreputable man, a rogue, held in contempt by everyone, is found as he lies dying. Suddenly those taking care of him manifest an eagerness, respect, even love, for his slightest sign of life. Everybody bustles about to save him, to the point, where, in the deepest coma, this wicked man senses something soft and sweet penetrating him [Aristotle's "beautiful day?"] ... Between his life and his death, there is a moment that is only that of a life playing with death ("Immanence: A Life," 28).

Even in animals, or rather, in our relation to animals, we distinguish between bare life and *a* life: animals are killed on mass, think of mass fishing, without committing a crime. But when residents along a coastline rush to save a few whales that have beached themselves, pushing and pulling them, watering their skin against the heat of the sun until the next tide comes in, what they respond to in each instance is *a* life, a single and singular life passing through this or that body of a giant animal.

The patient lying on the hospital bed, gasping for air, doctors bustling about him, is a patient-body, a sick-body wherein *a* life is combatting death. "The life of an individual gives way to an impersonal yet singular life that releases a pure event freed from the accidents of internal and external life . . . : 'Homo tantum.'" The life of an individuality (what Benjamin called "qualities" and "attributes") "fades away in favor of a singular life immanent to a man who no longer has a name" ("Immanence: A Life," 29).

This pure event is beyond the reach (re-territorialization) of every economy, calculation, measure, or comparison. It is something the political, biopolitical or not, cannot possibly grasp or touch, even if the medical personages, its agents or actors, respond to it instantaneously, intuitively, without necessarily understanding it. And when the political does touch it, when its relative value—relative to another life, to its utility or the life years it still has left to live—is measured on the scale of a point system of "last resort guidelines," then this pure event of *a* life is instantaneously converted into nothing more than bare life. When the ventilator is removed (or not) to help another patient survive, *both* become nothing more than bare life, more or less deserving to live according to a measured and measurable "merit."

Toronto, April 17, 2020

Postscript

Just as I finish drafting this text (without finishing with any of the questions the inventive virus keeps throwing at us, differently every day), Viktor Orbán of Hungary extends by decree the previously declared state of emergency, claiming indefinite powers for his office, indefinitely.

Hungary: is this final accomplishment of "illiberal" democracy a vindication *a posteriori* of Agamben's much criticized (rather than critiqued) contribution to the question? Did he foresee it, did he predict its coming? That the virus will be turned into a political weapon, and not only by Orbán, and become the pretext for the state of emergency becoming the normal form of government?

Once again, is it not just the form? (Form is relatively stable, but the content varies (Nietzsche)). Is it not just the form that is turned into a weapon, in the service not of a biopolitical regime carried to its very limit but, in the case of Hungary, of an archaic despotic kleptocracy? (Hungary has no experience of democratic forms of government, not even in its most reduced formalistic version now practiced elsewhere/everywhere.)

A Riposte

Instead of an exercise in biopower, the new political of Hungary stands in a relation of grotesque symmetry with that other regime of illimitation, that of Bolsonaro in Brazil, whose rhetoric incites public "incontinence"—promiscuous consumption, including the consumption by fire of the Amazon forest and its "river in the sky" that brings the rains to Africa.

What future path the globalized world will breach for itself, one cannot know. Whether it will try (in vain) to return the world to what it was just a few months ago (although it seems like a lifetime), or, worse, make the economy "roar" like a spruced-up car engine; or, on the contrary, it will learn the lesson this virus may teach us regarding the other existential crisis, which will not go away, even if we have almost lost sight of it in the midst of this immediate emergency? The lesson being: decarbonization is possible. The skies over Mumbai are blue again, the sea around Venice has been taken over by wildlife. Whether this lesson—mercilessly delivered by nothing more than a few strings of molecules, dormant, waiting for a life to come along to live—will be learnt, one cannot say. All that can be said is that what the "after" might be is yet to be determined.

Now this "viral" lesson, harsh and cruel as it may be, curiously resembles the divine justice of Benjamin. It does not spill blood, kills without leaving a trace of the act—in the interest of life. Without a trace: after the epidemic has passed and the generation responsible—if only through complicity—for the geocide on course will have been decimated, there will be no memory of the act. In the interest of life: perhaps it is a chance, perhaps the only chance, for another future for, made by, another (the "Greta") generation.

Agamben, the Virus, and the Biopolitical

1. There are several versions circulating in both English and French of Agamben's responses to the emergency measures imposed, in Italy in particular. The citation is from "Chiarimenti," first published in Italian on the blog *Quodlibet*, then republished on Medium. An authorized translation by Adam Kotsko, under the title "Clarifications," appeared in the *European Journal of Psychoanalysis*, which is my source here.
2. https://www.journal-psychoanalysis.eu/coronavirus-and-philosophers. Agamben's first interventions ("L'inventione di un'epidemia," and "Lo stato d'eccezione provocato da un'emergenza immotivata," February 26), subsequent clarifications ("Chiarimenti," March 17) and interviews circulate in several versions and lengths in Italian, in French and English translations, often under different titles (in *Quodlibet*, *Positions*, *Il Manifesto*, *Acta-zone*, *Marseille infos Autonomes*). "The Invention of an Epidemic" appeared in English translation (together with "Chiarimenti," or "Clarifications") in the *European Journal of Psychoanalysis*, where it was accompanied by a number of responses, including one by Jean-Luc Nancy, who dismisses it as "more like a diversionary manoeuvre than a political reflection." ("Viral Exception"). At https://www.journal-psychoanalysis.eu/coronavirus-and-philosophers.
3. "L'invenzione di un'epidemia," *Quodlibet*, February 26, 2020. At https://www.quodlibet.it/giorgio-agamben-l-invenzione-di-un-epidemia.
4. "Je ne suis ni virologue ni médicin." "L'épidémie montre clairement que l'état d'exception est devenu la condition normale," *Le Monde*, March 28, 2020.
5. According to the latest, in all likelihood, "conspiracy theory," it escaped from the P4 high-security bio-lab of Wuhan and from the control of the scientists or lab technicians who created it, or at least sought precisely to take charge of it, learn how to master it, to manipulate its code. This paranoid fantasy speaks to the dominant relation, even if it overestimates the power of science over life.
6. In this partial and selective destruction, the virus resembles the neutron bomb designed to kill only the living, while leaving (dead) infrastructure untouched. The virus, on the other hand, attacks the World, the living space of making (creating) sense, where sense circulates and is exchanged; it empties cities, theaters and the cinema; turns to deserts public spaces of gathering, of protestation, and mourning and celebration, where one makes an appearance, becomes visible . . . —all the while leaving/passing through other living forms (bats, pangolins) without leaving a trace.

A Riposte

7   This curious forgetting about the population would need to be reflected on at length. Here I can only defer to Foucault's argument (*The Birth of Biopolitics*) that in certain forms of neoliberalism economy detaches itself from society to enter into a reciprocal, symbiotic relation with the political: the political authorizes economic operations, which in turn legitimize the political. The excluded third, the social (health, welfare, housing, etc.), enters the ledger of negative expenditures.

Agamben, G. (1998) *Homo Sacer*, transl. by Daniel Heller-Roazen (Stanford: Stanford University Press).
Agamben, G. (2005) *State of Exception*, transl. by Kevin Attel (Chicago: University of Chicago Press).
Arendt, H. (1958) *The Human Condition* (Chicago: University of Chicago Press).
Benjamin, W. (1996) "Critique of Violence," in *Selected Writings, Vol. 1* (Cambridge, MA: Harvard University Press).
Deleuze, G. (2001) "Immanence: A Life," in *Pure Immanence: Essays on A Life*, transl. by Anne Boyman (New York: Zone Books).
Foucault, M. (1990) "Right of Death and Power over Life," *The History of Sexuality, Vol. 1*, transl. by Robert Hurley (New York: Vintage Books).
Foucault, M. (2008) *The Birth of the Biopolitics: Lectures at the Collège de France, 1978–79*, transl. by Graham Burchell (New York: Palgrave Macmillan).

Philosophy in the Time of the Epidemic: Two Transcripts

"Philosopher en temps d'épidémie": the syntagma serves as the title for the open series of critical reflections that Jérôme Lèbre (I suspect with the complicity of Jean-Luc Nancy) inaugurates on the first day of the confinement in France, on March 17.[1] It is difficult to render it in English, a language that (perhaps significantly?) lacks the verbal form for philosophy ("to philosophize" has altogether different, even negative connotations). Possible translations would need to rely on the mediation of an auxiliary verb (to do / to make philosophy) slowing down the impetus of the original—already an instance of (doing) philosophy, not an invitation or preparation for it. In place of a translation, I prefer to continue the thought and complete the sentence the syntagma launches: "(philosopher en temps d'épidémie) *so that there would be philosophy in the time of the epidemic.*" For nothing less than the continued presence of philosophy is at stake in the present, regarding our present, when the danger, as Hannah Arendt told us long ago, is that in disease and pain—to which conditions we should add panic and the fear of contamination—we would be thrown back upon our selves (the body, the privation of the "private," the home, the isolation of city, province, or even country . . .). Wittgenstein may have told us that it is a "fundamental misunderstanding" to try to understand pain by turning to the headache I have now, but this is precisely what is required of us today: to try to understand what is happening to us today by turning to the "here and now." Such timeliness we know is not a matter of course for philosophy, whose belatedness is structural. Turning (in the present to the present) takes up time. Yet it is precisely such a demand that Jérôme Lèbre makes (and he is not alone in taking on this responsibility[2]) when he sends out the invitation, indeed, issues the philosophical provocation to the "world" (that is, on the internet): "philosopher [which one could hear in the even stronger imperative mood of "philosophez!," engage in the practice of philosophy] en temps d'épidémie."

As for what philosophy should or could be in the time of the epidemic, the answer is developed in the course of the series itself: in the course of the practically daily postings of so far eighty video-recorded interventions, in several languages, arriving from all over the world . . . each of which responds differently to the title, each proposing or rather inventing a possible response, possibly co-constituting—by virtue of its singular difference—the plurality that is proper to philosophy, or in other words, ensuring that there would be philosophy in the time of the epidemic.

The time of the epidemic? At once the time of an emergency and of an exceptional urgency, also in the sense of Agamben's "exception(s)"—outside the law, yet held therein by the law. The emergency, a health crisis, is a condition, a facticity, imposed from the outside; the urgency, on the other hand, is interior to thought, philosophy, and writing.

In one of his several contributions to the series, Jean-Luc Nancy responds to the question "Où est l'urgence?," "Where is the urgency?[3] (in French emergency and urgency are signified by the same vocable). He "makes" cinema: onto a montage of borrowed images from a Western (*Stage Coach* I believe)—of horses, cowboys, "Indians," wildly chasing, crashing against one another—he grafts his own words, in his own voice: "Qui pousse?" Who pushes? What presses? What urges? he asks. Whence comes the "drive," "*Trieb*," "pulsion"? With regard, not to the world, the future of the world "after," but with regard to philosophy. The drive, the pulsion is "contemporaneity"—exceptionally, in the most literal sense possible in the time of the epidemic. It expresses itself as the urgency to write, the urge of immediacy, to be on time, here and now; to address and to be addressed without delay, to think and write contemporaneously with this extraordinary "now" (whose time still needs to be thought) in the simultaneous, even if virtual, co-presence of others. Deleuze called it the "society of friends."

As to the future, not of the world, but of this urgency itself, the question has not been—could not have been—asked before. For who would have thought that by June (this must be a short-hand designation, as such markers in the calendar say nothing in epidemic times) the *time* of the epidemic would have a "history." The shock of the early days, our sense that "Die Welt ist fort" (The world is gone), "the time is out of joint," has dissipated. The exceptional and the exception (in Agamben's sense) has installed itself for the duration (for how long?), have become normal without being normalized. In recognition of this mutation, this Journal *(EJP)* closes one of its two "tribunes," sends out a new invitation for new reflections on the subject of *Enduring Pandemic: Further Transmissions from Psychoanalysts & Philosophers.* Even before that Jérôme Lèbre changes the title of the series he curates: philosophy "in the time of the epidemic" becomes "philosopher au présent," philosophy "in the present."

What the writing of this new present becomes is, paradoxically, an affair of the future, of future writings yet to come. As for the writing dating from the past few months, "in the time of the epidemic," it has not been, it cannot be, surpassed. Prodigious, intense, immediate, the rich corpus is not "symptomatic" but a living testimony of the times. As I propose in one of my own interventions (#79)—the transcript of which is included here—this corpus composes a "disparate": a productive discursive heterogeneity that philosophy has remained in the time of the epidemic; a corpus that is held together in the plurality of its internal differences, without yielding to the tension of dispersion. In other words, without yielding to the greatest danger of the time: panic, fear, confusion.

The two interventions transcribed here with minor modifications reflect this heterogeneity. The first (#79) has become, after the fact, a sort of epilogue to the series, not just by virtue of the timing of its posting, just before the change of title closing the first series. It also recuperates as task, as urgency, the reconstitution of the very condition(s) for there being philosophy in the time of the epidemic.

The second (#66), on the other hand, is purely conceptual. It approaches the concept of bare life from another direction than the essay published earlier (in EJP) did.[4] It speaks in defense of the dignity of life—against the assault of the virus, and its categorical / conceptual equivalent, "bare life."

Transcript 1: "The title and its work(s)" #79, June 15, 2020[5]

"Philosopher en temps d'épidémie": I can attempt to answer this impossible challenge—invitation, incitation, or exhortation?—only indirectly, by way of a detour. Instead of addressing the title head on, I will turn here to the series of which this short video recording is itself a part: an open and open-ended chain of less than 15-minute-long video recordings *of* philosophy, in the same sense as one speaks of books *of* philosophy. Not works transposed or transferred to this medium after the fact, but works, miniatures really, created in and by and even for this medium. (Insofar as this writing here reverses this order and turns the "sayable" into something "readable," *a posteriori*, it cannot but bear the awkward marks of this translation.) In particular, I want to pay close attention to the extraordinary work the title performs, in the linguistic sense of this term, from outside the series it engenders—in just four words of a "syntagma," the fragment of a sentence.

Philosophy in the Time of the Epidemic

First, it indexes the doing of philosophy for its time, raising the question of its contemporaneity, or even stronger, making a demand for it, for turning the contemporaneity of its discourse into a question of/for philosophy. If Alain Badiou asks, *of what time are we the living witnesses in philosophy?*, then Jérôme's title here prompts me to ask, *not* how to do philosophy (*comment philosopher*) in the time of the epidemic, but rather how philosophy should or could let its discourse be marked by the living experience of this epidemic *as its time*, without either thematizing it, turning it into its subject or topic, or letting itself be contaminated by it (its fear, anxiety); without, that is, its discourse becoming either symptomatic or diagnostic of the epidemic. (For we recall what Heidegger said about diagnostic discourse: its time is of the eternal yesterday; its contemporaneity, entirely without us.)

Second, at the same time, and *in this same time* of the epidemic, the title opens a virtual plane on which to posit each contribution as one in a series of heterogeneous reflections, musings, mediations . . . which *the title at once engenders* (I would like to say, invites, liberates, sets free) and holds together in their *disparity* (Blanchot's term): standing in a relation of irreducible, plural differences, without yielding to the forces of dispersion. A singular multiple, thus.

When I chanced upon one of Jean-Luc Nancy's early contributions, and by consequence, learnt about the existence of this series and platform, I sent him a quick message: "I feel less alone." (I wonder if he recognized it as the same message that Jacques Derrida sent him after his (JLN) very first sending — a text, what else?) (Feeling) less alone? In relation to what? I've already asked this question regarding Derrida. Now it addresses me. Feeling less alone: in what sense does the *existence* of this platform (forum) and of the series (and not the content of its contributions) attenuate, lessen, my solitude? Surely not in the same sense that Facebook, Snapchat, Instagram, etc., bring to millions around the world relief from isolation in confinement and quarantine by offering their platforms as a substitute medium (literally a medium) for real-time exchanges and encounters.

As is often the case, it is Deleuze who helps me to answer my own questions. He names the two conditions for there to be philosophy, for its birth (which is every time): "Pour que la philosophie naisse" an encounter was necessary, "il a fallu une rencontre d'ami et de la pensée." For there to be philosophy an encounter was / is necessary between thought and friend. Against Hannah Arendt's *Life of the Mind* (thinking is a silent dialogue of the self with itself), Deleuze stages a *theatre* for thought; and in this theatre, philosophy does not give itself birth, either at its birth or later. It depends and continues to depend on a milieu. It passes in between: in the encounter between "thought" and (its) "friends," in the milieu of a "society of friends," with a taste for its discourse.

These conditions have never changed. My less than 15 minutes here also owe their possibility to a series of encounters—including the encounter with the title, as a performative. For its milieu, my intervention depends on what the platform (on Mediapart) virtually actualizes: it holds out the promise of a possible "society of friends," of complicity, which society in each of the eighty contributions makes itself present, presents itself, even if in a space that is virtual.

Although the series exists virtually and I am recoding this in my study, facing a camera that is looking at me without seeing me, this here is not a *substitute* for the real thing. It is not a *replacement for* the practice of philosophy but is precisely its doing, or (for one needs to be modest) a sort of doing philosophy, in the time of the epidemic: fabricating a discourse that is marked by it, contemporaneous with it, in the most literal sense of this term.

Just as I would conclude, a terrible idea (a notion, not a thought, only an idea) installs itself in me: what if the time is not that of an epidemic, which will pass, but the first (which is not even the first) in a cascade of never-ending catastrophes (collapses) yet to pass? What then of philosophy? What is philosophy to be in the time that remains?

Transcript 2: "Bare life: The poverty of the concept"[6] #66, May 28, 2020

Apropos the virus, but without mentioning its name, I will speak about the poverty of the *concept* of bare life: *poor-in-life*, poor as Heidegger's animal (not the concept but the lizard basking in the sun) is "poor-in-world," *weltarm*.

Poor (in life): means not flawed, weak, or impotent; that the concept would be powerless to conjure up a possible world (as Deleuze demands of a concept). On the contrary, it is twice implicated in a powerful *productive* operation with a long history, dating back to the Greeks, at least as far as Aristotle, which operation will permit Agamben to recast the whole history of the political of the west as the fabrication of bare life . . .

The first operation is the decision to cut (which as Derrida reminds us is the etymological root of decision); to insert the cut of a schism into life, which it reconstitutes / reinvents as life divided into two heterogeneous domains: two (domains), for to say "bare life" or "zoe" or "blosse Leben," etc., is also to say—simultaneously and silently—"good," "qualified," or "just life." For this cut is also a measure. Like the scale of justice, it measures the relative value of what it has just created. So that Benjamin could write: it is ignoble to claim that the bare life in man is worth more than a just life; so that philosophy could refuse to reject the death penalty: there must be something worth dying for (see Derrida on this point); so that Agamben could show disdain for the Italians who willingly surrender every political value, cling onto mere life, in fear of infection, disease, or death.

Second, the concept "bare life" is itself a powerful operator. Across genealogical layers of history, of cultural, geographical, class, etc., differences, it gathers together into this one figure (called "homo sacer" in the book with the eponymous title): the migrant, the refugee, the "sans abri," the "black lives (that) matter," the terrorist, the addict-body abandoned in the back alley, the old and infirm dying in care homes, the body kneeling on Boulevard Saint Michel with a sign: "j'ai faim"; the Roma, the Rohingya, the inmates of Gulags, Auschwitz, Guantanamo . . .

Yet the poverty of the concept is of a different order than that of its referents. It is structural. Something other than existence escapes it, something other than what can be *extracted / wrenched away* from life. Except that "escape" may not be the right term here. In any case, not in the same sense that the virus escapes *from* captivity *to* the "wild," both the real (space) and the concept: leaps over the divide human / animal, deterritorializes from nature / reterritorializes itself on the World. It would be more precise to say that something other than *existence* (for life is an encounter of forces, of intensities, whereas existence is static, as it were "lifeless") does not escape the concept, but falls outside the plane or field of its operation. Here Heidegger's animal (again, the lizard and not the concept) is instructive: the lizard does not *suffer* from a lack in World, it itself is the absence of any possible relation to the World. With regard to life, this something, which I cannot yet name, but whose name I know is neither *zoe* nor qualified life, is not simply missing / missed after the great division / decision. Instead, its very place falls away.

Ironically, it is Aristotle, the great divider, who designates it with great precision, even if he prefaces it with the qualifier "as if":

If there is no great difficulty as to the way of life [*kata ton bion*], clearly most men will tolerate much suffering and hold onto life (*zoe*) as if it were a kind of serenity [*euemereia*, beautiful day] and a natural sweetness.

If we disregard this "as if," not regard it as if it were casting doubt upon the reality of the "beautiful day" and "natural sweetness," or upon what Glenn Gould characterized as what matters in Bach's method of composition, in its endless detours, delays, and refusal to reach the end, the "joyous essence of being"—then Aristotle points to what is excluded by the founding gesture. What remains after the great division of the life-world unaccounted for is the "beautiful day" that neither register—neither *bios* (qualified life) nor *zoe* (bare life)—can accommodate.

Today, more than ever it seems, we need to return to this unaccounted-for remainder; especially today, in the time of this epidemic. We need to recuperate it from its exile underground, as we—not just the Italians but the whole world—tremble in the face of a globalizing threat to life in each and every one of us.

The question then is how to rescue what necessarily falls in between, exists in the gap between life's nakedness and its full qualification (person, personality, the singularity of its quality), between political life and bare life? How to rescue by way of a concept or concepts the sweetness Aristotle spoke of, and rescue it as irreducible to fear (of death), to instinct (for survival), clinging onto life at any cost (which earns Agamben's contempt and Benjamin's characterization as ignoble)? How to rescue that element or dimension—but then what is the right word here? Is it not sense?—the *sense* (in every sense of this word) of life, whose "non-existence would be something more terrible" (says Benjamin) than any "attained" condition of man?

The body clinging onto the side of an overcrowded inflatable, the body that makes one last effort to cross the desert, is bare

Two Transcripts

life: standing in a relation, even in its absolute solitude and abandonment. It is a creation, a product manufactured by the machinery of a political that expelled it precisely from the world into which it was born. In fact, from the World itself. Outside the law but held by the law outside the World. On the other hand, what *Aquarius* and the other rescue ships are searching for in the open sea, what the volunteers combing the desert of Texas for refugees hope to save, is a third category of living existence. Deleuze gave it the simple name: *a* life.

> No one has described better what a life is than Charles Dickens ... A disreputable man, a rogue, held in contempt by everyone, is found as he lies dying. Suddenly those taking care of him manifest an eagerness, respect, even love, for his slightest sign of life. Everybody bustles about to save him, to the point, where, in the deepest coma, this wicked man senses something soft and sweet penetrating him [Aristotle's "beautiful day"?] ... Between his life and his death, there is a moment that is only that of a life playing with death. ("Immanence: A Life")

Even in animals, or rather, in our relation to animals, we distinguish between bare life and *a* life: animals are killed on mass, think of mass fishing, without committing a crime. But when residents along a coastline rush to save a few whales that have beached themselves—pushing and pulling them, watering their skin against the heat of the sun until the next tide comes in—what they respond to in each instance is *a* life, a single and singular life passing through this or that body of a giant animal.

The patient lying on the hospital bed, gasping for air, doctors bustling about him, is a patient-body, a sick-body wherein *a* life is combatting death. "The life of an individual gives way to an impersonal yet singular life that releases a pure event freed from the accidents of internal and external life ... : 'Homo tantum.'" The life of an individuality (what Benjamin called "qualities" and "attributes") "fades away in favor of a singular life immanent to a man who no longer has a name."

This pure event is beyond the reach (re-territorialization) of every economy, calculation, measure, or comparison. It is something the political, biopolitical or not, cannot possibly grasp or touch, even if the medical personages, its agents or actors, respond to it instantaneously, intuitively, without necessarily understanding it. And when the political does touch it, when its relative value—relative to another life, to its utility or the life years it still has left to live—is measured on the scale of a point system of "last resort guidelines," then this pure event of *a* life is instantaneously converted into nothing more than bare life. When the ventilator is removed (or not) to help another patient survive, *both* become nothing more than bare life, more or less deserving to live according to a measured and measurable "merit."

---

1 *Philosopher en temps d'épidémie.* Une chaine proposée par Jérôme Lèbre. Avec le soutien de la Maison des Écrivains et de la Littérature. Announcement of the series on March 17, 2020,
https://www.youtube.com/watch?v=vycLdnQGhjk&t=73s.

2 The *European Journal of Psychoanalysis*, on whose virtual pages this text first appeared, opened two "tribunes" with the aim of immediately responding to the "global Coronavirus pandemic, considered along the axes of psychoanalysis and philosophy": *Psychoanalysts Facing Coronavirus* and *Coronavirus & Philosophers*. Joseph Cohen opens his video communications, in the form of interviews, under the heading "Antivirus philosophiques" from Monaco. Some daily papers and popular publications (*Le Monde, Libération*, the Italian *Quodlibet*, where Agamben's provocative interventions first appeared) also opened their pages to philosophical reflections or at least reflections by philosophers.

3 "Oú est l'urgence? (1)": "Video in 3 parts broadcast starting from May 11, 2020, the day when in France and in other countries strict confinement was partially lifted." At
https://www.youtube.com/watch?v=3hf1fjM5VO8.

4 Zsuzsa Baross, "Agamben, the Virus, and the Biopolitical: A Riposte." Revised version included in this volume. First published by *EJP*, posted

Two Transcripts

May 12, 2020. At http://www.journal-psychoanalysis.eu/agamben-the-virus-and-the-biopolitical-a-riposte. Republished in *Coronavirus, Psychoanalysis, and Philosophy* (2021). Eds. Fernando Castrillon and Thomas Marchevsky, London: Routledge.

5   Zsuzsa Baross, "Le titre et son travail / The title and its works(s)," intervention #79. At https://www.youtube.com/watch?v=qqOKcQjVBiw

6   Zsuzsa Baross, "Vie nue: la pauvreté du concept / Bare life: The poverty of the concept," intervention # 66. At https://www.youtube.com/watch?v=oh2Tq1NtIAw

On the Absence of the World, One More Time; Or, Finding the World, Again

Preamble

Here is the last verse of the short poem *Grosse, Blühende Wölbung* by Paul Celan:[1]

> *Die Welt ist fort, ich muss dich tragen.*

"The world is gone, I must carry you." Two discrete phrases, absolutely heterogeneous discursive units: the one is a *constat*, a statement of fact, the other an injunction that commands. At once separated and, in their dissonance, joined together to form a single line by the typographical mark of a comma, they themselves become carriers. In excess of their referents, today they bear (*tragen*) a series of disconcerting questions regarding "You" and "I" in the world: who (which one of "us") is addressing "You" in the accusative form of "Dich" in the first person as "I"? Who (among us) is brought together, face-to-face in the world, by the sheer force of these words in this nonreciprocal, asymmetrical relation of duty and obligation vis-à-vis "You"? Who is to occupy the one and the other vacant subject position readymade by these personal pronouns, waiting for us to be addressed there by Celan's words, even before we will have arrived? And where "there," when the world is gone? And whose world is gone, departed, lost, absent or absenting itself? And where on earth (as asks the common idiom) in the world should "I" carry "You" when the world is gone?

I
2019, Paris

"Die Welt ist fort, ich muss dich tragen." I first cite this double phrase of Celan in early 2019, well before the arrival of the virus and the time of this pandemic.[2] It was a difficult missive to receive, to hear properly, even then. The first unit, at once a statement and a sentence in the juridical sense, passes a terrible judgment on the state / fate of the world: it is "gone." The second pronounces a cruel, if not impossible imperative: "I must carry you." And if the weight of the burden of each were not difficult enough to bear (*tragen*), the comma in between places us at the point of their conjunction: commending or condemning (me? us?) to carry "you" (who remains unnamed) when the world (whose world?) is gone.

I am citing Celan in the text, but in the writing I am reading Derrida, especially closely his last seminar, where, after *Béliers*[3] and other texts, he returns to the last verse of this "short and great poem."[4] I am thus reading Celan with and through the writing of Derrida, which more than ever yields to the rhythm of the living discourse of the seminar. In the course of this time perhaps excessively long *séances* (they will be the last, as he probably knows, and despite the promise to return to a subject the following year, there will be no next time[5]), it systematically maps out and, with infinite patience, pursues, tracks down, the elusive, plural, proliferating sense of this single line.

It is thus Derrida who brings me to Celan. I am reading the last verse apropos, before I would be reading it by way of Derrida. As always, the writing bedazzles with its virtuosity, its apparent mastery over the countless bifurcations it opens, the swarms of significations it liberates, starting with the two keys

On the Absence of the World, One More Time

terms of the poem. "Fort" is made to migrate between departure, withdrawal, absence, loss . . . (of the world); whereas "tragen"—in plurilingual translations of the polysemous German word—is itself made to carry [*tragen*] the sense of the French *porter*, *supporter*, *transporter*, the English to carry, to bear, and, via its complex semantic links to Heidegger's German, "Austrag" and the even more distant "Walten."[6]

But fascination this time is accompanied by a new sensation, the sense of a disconcerting dislocation that, simultaneously with its vertiginous hermeneutics, the seminar speaks to me in a different tongue this time; it is addressing me differently, from another space, another time, from the other side of a fault line. It strikes me—I have the intuition, the sensible certitude as I am re-reading it in 2019 (I use this date, which also heads this section, as shorthand and index for an order of time whose character is not yet clear at the time of the writing, and in fact will become its very question)—that the referent of the word "world" (*Welt*) in Celan's enunciation has shifted (redoubled over itself) since the time of the seminar, even since its publication as a text, not even a decade ago. It has come to refer to (while still speaking of the *Welt* of Celan), has come to regard (*regarde*) the seminar itself, and by extension, the corpus, the voice, the figure "Derrida" as whose world is gone, departed, lost. And while this mutation (redoubling) takes place in the space of the writing, its location and milieu, this time it is not the work of the writing. Indeed, it necessarily exceeds and escapes it as its posthumous after-effect belatedly actualized in the performative repetition of my re-reading, in another order of time.

As for this other order—of time and world, of a world-time at an unsurpassable distance from the time of the seminar, 2003 in calendar time—my contemporaries still struggle to name it, to define precisely its radical alterity, as "other." They variably give it as "epoch without an epoch" (Bernard Stiegler); *a* time of "mutation," still in historical time (Jean-Luc Nancy in the strategically entitled, *Que faire);* the time of *effondrement* (the diagnosis of the school of "collapsology"). The most dramatical nomination, the time of *"the* geocide," comes from the poet-philosopher, Michel Deguy. Notwithstanding the divergences, even *différends*, the diagnoses resonate (resound))with the sentence Celan passes on the fate of the world, perhaps even gesture toward it as precursor. They say differently that a world is gone, that they speak *in* a world "after" *of* a "world after" from the other side of an abyssal hiatus. Badiou even names the present "temps intervallaire," "time of the interval,"

"2019" heading this section is thus a temporal index for a writing reading Derrida in a present (already not the same as the time of the writing here) cut off from the time of the seminar, from world-time when we were reading Celan, Heidegger, Benjamin . . . , indeed the whole Western canon with Derrida; when we were still reading Derrida (almost) at the same time as he was writing his texts and seminars; when *we* (Derrida and us) still cohabited the world as the same world in common, whose future, we thought, we still had in common and to which—notwithstanding catastrophes, disappointments, reversals . . . —he could (still ask us to) say "yes." Unconditionally.

The "world after": that is to say, after the world that (Derrida's) deconstrunctions silently assume as their ground, *fond*, *terre*, *sol*, is "fort," gone, absent . . . —which is also to say, simultaneously: after the verse of Celan repositions us and, (re)assigning the subject positions—the "I" (*ich*) and the "You" (*dich* in the accusative case)—burdens me / us with the task, imposing on me / us the impossible obligation and difficult duty to carry (*tragen*). it is I / we who now must transport the figure, the voice, the missive, the corpus "Derrida" to "here and now," make it our contemporary in / of this world that itself is lacking full presence, is departing, collapsing, destituting itself.

Such was not the conclusion but the point of reasoned departure for the first volume *On Contemporaneity, after Agamben*.[7] This text here may serve as a belated postscript to it or, alternatively and

/ or simultaneously, become the untimely preface to the next volume *On the Time that Remains*—yet to be written, or again, given the order of time that is the "now," perhaps never to be written.

II (a)
Toronto, Summer / Fall, 2020

I am writing this in the time of the epidemic, in yet another order of time. Or as I should rather say, I am beginning to write, for I cannot know if or when I will be able to finish, if I will have the time, whether the epidemic will give me / leave me the time, or again, whether it will finish first or will outlast my time, or, even worse, will never finish with its time. Indeed, there are signs already that its *time* has mutated, acquired a "history." The first shock of astonishment regarding the impossible—"time is out of joint," "die Welt ist fort"—has dissipated; the epidemic has installed itself for the duration (for how long?). (Just recently, two of the several platforms[8] that have responded to the immediacy of the urgency as the urgency to write, for writing to be on time, to be contemporaneous with this epidemic time, have adjusted the temporal index in their titles: Jérôme Lèbre's electronic YouTube *chaîne* "Philosopher en temps d'épidémie" has become "Philosopher au temps présent"; while the *Journal of European Psychoanalysis* opened a new "tribune": *Enduring Pandemic: Further Transmissions from Psychoanalysts & Philosophers*.) The time of "exception" has become normal without being normalized.

The time of the epidemic: a curious time. A "drôle de temps" (after Sartre's "drôle de guerre," a war without fighting a war): a time, a temporality, whose time is not passing. A suspended, arrested time (if *in* time, in what *ord*er of time?), or, more precisely perhaps, a peculiar instance of time's involution that evokes the (still) image of Hokusai's famous *Great Wave*. It rises into mid-air but never completes its downward descent to crash into the foaming waters below. Or an even better metaphor perhaps is served up by the "arrested, frozen wave, with the curve and the foam on the crest" that so impressed the cineaste Alain Fleischer in the harbor of Reykjavik.[9] As he hypothesizes, the wave could not have been formed in an instant, all at once, but was built wave by wave, each new wave adding a fresh layer of ice to what must have been just a grain at first, but which already blocked the waves' passage. This moving image (Fleischer is after all a cinematographer; he even tries to replicate the effect in *La Vague Gelée*, 1997) better captures the sense of this epidemic time, at once in movement and paralyzed, movement in paralysis. A thickening, a densification of the present, to which Instants from the future continue to arrive but cannot pass to the past, blocked as they are by an arrested present still occupying their place. As if the active synthesis of time—for which the present functions as a point of passage, contracting at once with the instant passing to the past and the future yet to come—was arrested mid-way. Successive presents are crowding together in the same place, piling up on one another, without contracting into a flux, into a time that passes. The next wave and the next instant recoil before the future ahead, blocking its passage in mid-stream. A new temporality is thus born; for time still temporalizes but gives birth to a perhaps never-before experienced "presentism." The inversion of what has been not even a month ago our dominant relation to time. Facilitated, willed, imposed by technology, it has devoured the future and obliterated the past in a perpetually extended and, paradoxically, accelerated present; in contrast, this epidemic is a slow time, of waiting, waiting for the present (confinement, contagion, the danger of infection) to pass. Will it ever pass? we ask anxiously. Will the / a future ever come to pass? Will there be an exit from this unending time? And if yes, to what order of time? Will the same world-time as before be awaiting us at the other end? ("Reboot" is a term often used.) Or it will be the same, only worse, as Michel Houellebecq has predicted.[10] Or, on the contrary, we have entered a wholly other order of time, and it has already appropriated to its history this present epidemic as one in a cascade of catastrophes, both past and yet to come?

A time without events. There are peaks and ebbs, the curve of new infections now rises then flattens, before rising again; "hot spots" flare up, "waves" begin, spread from "clusters" to whole cities, to cantons, provinces, and continents . . . then to the globe itself. All the while, nothing happens, nothing passes, which is another justification for calling it a "phony" time. Time is nothing, Bergson taught us, unless it is doing something. True, there is a state of emergency, but it is without urgency: no mad rush, feverish panic, frenetic agitation, or call to action. On the contrary, the call or order is for inaction, immobility: do not move; stay at home; lock yourself in; keep your distance. Yes, scientists are urgently searching for the antidote, the vaccine. But are they looking for it in the right place (on the surface of the virus or inside the cell)? And will it come?[11] Will it work, be safe, give full or only partial immunity? For how long? Even more importantly, how to live until then? If there is an "until then," if there is a time to come "after," if we are not living already in the time "after." What would "the livable life of life" be, "la vie vivable de la vie" (Duras),[12] until then? For those who will not live until then, for whom this epidemic time is all that remains to live? These uncertainties (Jean-Luc Nancy: "certitude trembles," "we are exiting of the era of certainty"[13]) only reinforce our immobility.

For passive we are. As Blanchot writes, "we are passive in relation to (*par rapport*) the disaster."[14] Except, our passivity is not a relation, which, as Jean-Luc Nancy often reminds us ("pas de rapport sans écart"), requires a distance, the distancing of a gap, an interval, without which, as we will see, there can be no world. No world can "world" (to borrow Heidegger's neologism turning the noun into a verb) without the gaps / interstices / intervals that run through the tissue of the world, and which interstices are not empty, idle, or unproductive spaces. They are modulators of distance and proximity, operators that rhythmically structure (differentiate / heterogenize) space, are productive of what Foucault called "other" spaces. Intervals cut lines of communications into space, compose the infinitely complex web of linkages that hold up the tissue of the world, the tissue that the world is. For this same reason, "catastrophe" would be a better term than "disaster," which is spectacular, evokes images of wild destruction from the outside, earthquakes, tsunamis, hurricanes, fires . . . , whereas catastrophe, as the collapse of coordinates on the interior (in the mathematico-geometrical sense of discontinuity caused by continuity) is a silent event. Indeed, the material world outside my window looks much the same as before, as if after a neutron bomb event. Physical structures are intact, but the streets in between are silent, empty of bodies, without movement. Inside this zone, time (if it still merits the name) is without signposts. Missing from the world are the markers necessary for orientation, finding direction, fixing one's location in time: future and past, before and after, tomorrow, last week, the day before. The distinctions between yesterday and tomorrow, past and future—is this next week already?—become blurred, lose their sense as pure sensation. Yet, it is these markers that give us the sense of time, are the sensible condition of the experience, as sensation, of time. The sense of time: its color ("one emerged from the gray of the night" [Paul Klee]), its season and its seasoning ("La matinée était très sucrée" [Paul Morand]). In the conference presentation "Voir le temps venir"[15] ("To see time to come") that predates the pandemic, Nancy speaks toward—and only toward, for the infinite richness of time cannot be recuperated—its coming and going; return and repetition; its passage and taking place; it being countable or propitious time (of the now); or having a duration in time . . . Perhaps for the first time, ever so briefly, he also touches on the "season" and the "seasoning" of time: a time in the cycle of the year or the day and its taste or flavor (as in seasoning with herbs and spices a dish one prepares). But this time, this present in the "here and now" lacks not only these qualities. (Sunday has lost its shine and nothing enters from the grayness of the night, no fire, nothing "wrapped in blue floats over icefields." It is because of this nothing, that nothing, no color emerges from it, that Delacroix may have called "grey the enemy of painting.") Exceptionally this time, time also lacks the properties "proper" to time: progression, passage, and delay; belatedness and being in advance; departure and arrival; rhythm and pulsation... Amorphous and homogeneous, it has no structure, no shape. Like molasses or the subatomic particle X, the Higgs boson that gives matter its mass, it resists passage. The passage of time itself and our passage through it.

What World corresponds with this time, as its other face and reverse side? For time is also world, world-time, says Derrida ("Time: it is *le temps*, but also *l'histoire*, and it is *le monde*, time, history, world"[16]). What history could be still written by this suspended, non-productive time? What world still worlds, to ask again with Heidegger, what "Welt weltet" in a time empty of events, suspended but without the suspense of events, of a future to come (*un avenir à venir*)?

On the socio-anthropological plane, in the register of "civilization," of techno-scientific culture, the virus "serves nothing," as Jean-Pierre Dupuy replies to his interlocutor.[17] It brings no revelations; it is not the "inessential manifestation of essence," as Gérard Bensoussan proposes, after Hegel.[18] It is questionable whether this epidemic is an "event" at all in the proper sense, or that it brings to light the "insisting presence of death" at the heart of our projects, as Jean-Luc Nancy claims.[19] It discloses no metaphysical truths or even "social facts" (in Durkheim's definition) that we did not or could not or should not have known: the ruthless logic of the globalized economic order; the chasms that run through the social body between rich and poor, black and white, immigrant and native, suburb and inner city, front-line ("essential") work and *télétravail*, the young and the old . . . ; the pitiful state of our hospitals, health-care systems, care homes, prisons . . . Nor does it deliver lessons yet to be learnt regarding our catastrophically destructive relation to what we still call the "environment," "nature," or the "planet" . . .

Still, there is a massive "virus effect": a threefold humiliation inflicted on the world, which is not a moral lesson in humility (again as Bensoussan would suggest), but a massive "narcissistic wound," to borrow Avital Ronell's term, three times delivered.

i.

The first time it is inflicted on the self-image of the "man of our age," on the "mankind of modern civilization" of whom Freud (in *Civilization and its Discontents*, 1930) already declared: "he has almost become a god himself . . . When he puts on all his auxiliary organs"—the still modest telegraph, telephone, radio, etc., in comparison with the "exo-organs" (Stiegler) attached to / implanted / grafted onto the body of his successor, the so-called "posthuman"—he "is truly magnificent."[20] Three decades after Freud, Blanchot ("On a Change of Epoch [1960]"[21]) reaches back to Teilhard's techno-romanticism of the same epoch and to Jünger, who is already writing of the atomic age, to conjure up (one does not quite know whether with approval or approbation) the latest prototype of this man as the man of "lack of measure." Propelled onto breaching paths to infinite, unlimited progress, this "man has become a sun, who seizes the constitutive forces of nature," embarks on an "extreme adventure of unforeseen consequences," and "each time Mother Earth begins to tremble [. . .] is able to take this shaking in hand and capture it."[22]

These figures, as we know, are not the first, not the inventors of the invention of reinventing the world. They have ancient precursors, are the creative mutations of Homer's (invention of) the "man of many wiles," whose calculative logic Adorno and Horkheimer blamed for or placed at the origin of the "disenchantment" of the world. There is a long history, passing through Descartes and Heidegger, modern science and politics, to this project of (re)creating the World as ours alone, not just unshared but unshareable with all other (living) thing (classed as either "worldless" or "poor in world").

And yet, this World closed upon itself has always been open to the skies, albeit differently conceived, even perceived. Today's successors of the ancients have blasted open the vault, literally, to look back in time at the origin of the universe: of light and of time itself. Tracing in reverse rays that reach us only now from the immemorial past, they have almost touched the birth of light (time) itself.

Just a few weeks ago, the world, at least a small world (including the President, especially the President, eager to show off the private nature of the enterprise) enthusiastically celebrated the launch of the SpaceX capsule taking, after the hiatus of many decades, American astronauts to the International Space Station. (In defiance—or was it rather méconnaissance or denegation? —of the virus, they did not distance or wear masks.) The spectacle was bound to disappoint those who sought a repetition of the "original" jubilant experience of the heroic epoch of the Apollo mission. Not that there was any need for it. There have been far greater, far more "magnificent" achievements than this "taxi-service" since: the spacecraft Rosetta was sent to catch up with the comet Tchouri, an object travelling on a trajectory in a wholly other space–time, from the beginning of time. No calculation, no measure in (earth) years and miles, could possibly apprehend this encounter for human imagination. Still, the last photograph, a glimpse that Rosetta captured of the site / sight of the lander Philae on the rocky surface of the comet, may compensate for this failure of poetics by space sciences. It is, one must admit, of exceptional poetic beauty: a fragile metal object, barely visible, is caught in the shadow of a crevice. One of Philae's three thin legs is stretched out as if to be illuminated for this one photograph by the faint light still reaching it from the sun. A "folie," like the madness of useless architectural objects planted in gardens and parks. Or a fossil of human technology now on its eternal journey deep into the universe, until the end of time or of the comet, when its ball of ice is burnt up by a sun. After which Philae would continue with its journey, all alone. A precursor of future art, or art in the time that remains?

The SpaceX mission is almost banal in comparison. For the new protagonist is no longer the man of infinite progress (faster, lighter, cheaper), breaching the path of a limitless, continuous progression. The new figure, "limitrophic," takes up residence on the limit, or, even more transgressively, turns the limit into a springboard for leaping to other "spaces": the red shift (a distortion of vision) becomes the means to detect the (invisible) movement and expansion of the universe; the gravitational field of planets serves to lob spacecrafts, against their own gravitational force, onto new trajectories leading to even more distant objects; the new man of science "listens" to the gravitational shock waves that ripple through space–time, searching for events that passed billions of years ago inside black holes: the invisible / the impenetrable par excellence... This figure is thus closer to Ulysses who defeats the gods by outwitting them and represents a break with the inventors of war machines, of propulsion engines, of everything that meets force with an even greater force.[23]

Yet, it is this "man," the collective subject of spectacular adventures and accomplishments, without precedent in the history of the universe (if we may assume, by hypothesis, that we are all alone and the stage of this spectacle is the universe), that the virus shows up as impotent, leaving him with no other means of self-defense than a flimsy cloth mask, forcing him to retreat from the world and exile himself in the "oikos," the space of privation treated with contempt by the Greeks. The other protection, the vaccine, if successful, takes time, takes up the duration of our living time. Unmanipulable, incompressible, it must be lived through. Meanwhile, "it"—a mere nanometric "thing," a "virus without quality"[24] whose status as a living entity is itself questionable, composed of only RNA molecules—brings the whole world of global humanity, in the first truly global catastrophe experienced as such to a halt. Even more humiliatingly, it brackets (in the phenomenological sense of suspension) the "magnificent," the "spectacular" and "groundbreaking" overcoming of the limit. With the backward move of an "après coup," it qualifies man's omnipotence and magnificence by exposing the "fragility of the skin of the world" (the title of Jean-Luc Nancy's recent book[25]), the limit condition, as that which has never changed. True, he knew that he was standing on Earth (he) devastated, but he could at least console himself with having acquired the powers of the sun, to have become the creator of matter and time, of subatomic particles of ephemeral durations, in earth time, for the first time.

He, who may have dreamt of / planned his escape by colonizing other planets, now finds himself failing, falling into a maelstrom, away from the world (of men).

One could understand Agamben's outrage[26] over the passivity of the collective acceptance of this humiliation, as one could also understand the anti-mask protests in the name of "liberty"—provided that the target of this irrationally rational / rationally irrational gesture was not the political, itself at loss, outwitted, outrun by the virus, but the virus itself. In this case, the protest may even remind us of Voltaire protesting the irrationality of nature devastating Lisbon in the massive 1755 earthquake. Agamben is right: the states of emergency in force all over the world amount to a passive acceptance of and surrender to impotence. Even more so than Agamben believes it to be the case. For the notion that the state of emergency is a political stratagem in the service of a totalitarian tendency to suspend the law and normal rule of government attributes power over the virus and the potency of action to at least a certain class of political agents. Whereas, if we concede, as I suggest elsewhere in this volume,[27] that the drastic measures (lockdown, quarantine, closure, surveillance) are the last line of defense by an impotent political, then what is at stake is not individual survival "at any cost" but the survival of the political itself. Not of this or that government or regime but of the body politic, the world constituted as a political body and the world politically constituted as a body.

Nonetheless, the state of exception is doubly biopolitical.

First, the self-defense of last resort is an autoimmune reaction (in Derrida's rigorous definition of the term). By virtue of its own logic, it turns against, destroys the very body it intends to protect. Curiously, in this overdrive it also mimics the overreaction to the virus of the biological body. Except that the political is well capable of recognizing itself. It is *à son corps défendant,* in the uncannily appropriate French idiom, at once despite itself *and* in self-defense that it attacks its own tissue: the interconnected, rhizomatic networks of proximity, touch, encounter, inter-course . . . that constitute, to borrow once again a terminology from Heidegger, the world of World-building (*Weltbildend*) man. The grotesque irony of this post-age epidemic is that the one (being / Dasein) who embarks on journeys of unforeseen consequence, who dares as a latter-day Prometheus to steal the powers of the sun, falls victim / fails against a "virus without quality," which forces him to seek the safety of banal domesticity.

The second purely biopolitical aspect of the confinement—contrary to the claim made by those who cite Foucault's *Discipline and Punish* as their evidence—is that the modern biopolitical is dedicated to life (or, as one could say with Benjamin, to "bare life"), its founding principle being that the administration and management of the life of the population is the political task par excellence. Death for such regimes is an embarrassment, a failure, as Foucault tells us in the earlier text appended to *The History of Sexuality*.[28] The mass deaths in care homes, in the neighborhoods of minorities and the poor, death by hundreds of thousands in whole states, only expose the humiliating impotence and incompetence of biopolitical regimes.

ii.

The second order of humiliation is inflicted on the most elementary form of *sense*. Not on common sense in its common usage, a faculty of sound judgment in navigating the practical affairs of the world; nor on "bon sens," whose equal distribution among men in the world Descartes assumes as axiomatic. It is not even Hannah Arendt's "sensus communis"—a discursively accomplished shared sense of the world as shared, as the *same* world seen from different perspectives—that is humiliated, but the precondition of all these. What is just a *"sense."* Like pain or hunger, impossible to negate or doubt. It has force, it enforces itself. One may call it a "sensible certitude" (again in Benoussan's borrowing of Hegel), a certitude so certain that its case paradoxically cannot be made, argued for or demonstrated. It can only be pointed to, could only be a *geste*, a performative: "look!" Therein lies also its fragility. When questioned, when, against every sense, it is denied, it cannot defend itself nor can it be defended.

To further complicate matters, the humiliation inflicted on this primitive sense by the virus is of a second order. It arrives to a sense already humiliated. When its inherent fragility is amply demonstrated, impotently experienced, and openly displayed, indeed, flaunted in the world; when nonsense sticks like molasses to the sense of the "real" and to the real as a "sense"; when collective hypnoses successfully resist, neutralize, render impotent argument, demonstration, evidence, with 'l'évidence" that is obvious in and by itself; when the latest mutations of "grotesque power" (Foucault) and the "tyranny of buffoons" (Salmon[29]) have effectively rendered laughter, irony, parody, farce, and comedy—the power of the grotesque: itself a sense—feeble (including Badiou's philosophical riposte: "comedy is a thought of the present"[30]); when the infinitely resourceful and productive machines of the false have successfully appropriated to themselves even the terms "false," "fake," "faux" . . .

Nothing, that is, except the virus. Where science, reason, argument, evidence, persuasion, demonstration, protest, contestation, revelation . . . even experience, have all failed, the virus is succeeding, albeit not without difficulties and reversals. It is establishing in the continuous present its cruel truth. Truth by numbers—the exponential explosion of infections, hospitalizations, incubations, and deaths—and by the infection of the great falsificators (Trump, Bolsanaro) themselves. Where the "sense" of the real and the reality of sense have failed, the virus—as Benoussan suggested—renders justice. Not to ideas, not to the idea of truth or justice. Only to the facticity of facts—which, in this epoch, is not nothing.[31]

iii.

The third humiliation, purely a moral one, is selective. For the virus is selective. It appears to act in the world as if another invisible hand, which, on the one hand, prosecutes a program of eugenics, on the model of familiar fascist ideologies; and on the other, administers (in the absence of the divine) a cruel and crude "natural" justice. The first "hand" promotes the survival of the fittest and targets for elimination the weakest and the most vulnerable: the sick, the immuno-compromised, but also the undocumented migrants, farm workers, "black and brown people" in general. It especially, and especially ruthlessly, kills those unproductive by virtue of age—the old. (Curiously, in its form, this injustice resembles the justice of Walter Benjamin's divine violence that strikes without warning, kills without spilling blood and leaves no trace. People die alone and out of sight. There are no rituals around the corpse, no funerals, no communal mourning. Corpses disappear, unceremoniously, without witnesses, into the fire of public crematoria.[32])

The viral justice meted out by the other "hand" has little to do with the difficult death, which is visited, more or less randomly, on many of the sick. Its humiliation—if humiliation could be considered justice, if justice could humiliate—is reserved for the old: the generation that is implicated in this viral catastrophe and cannot consider itself objectively innocent, as the helpless victim of a purely bio-hazard event. It bears a collective responsibility and moral liability for what we still call a "climate crisis," despite it being man-made, and of which this epidemic is both a consequence and a manifestation. This will be, as Isabelle Stengers predicts, the most hated generation "in human memory."[33] The generation that "'knew' but did nothing or too little . . . [but] which will avoid the worst of catastrophic times and will be already dead."[34]

The humiliation is not that this safe assumption may turn out to have been very wrong. It is not fear either, the fear of living what remains of life in the fear of an almost certain death sentence, in the case of infection, or, if not yet touched by it, of living in constant fear of it, a life reduced to nothing but (bare) life. Viral justice takes a different course: it reverses the direction of "intergenerational solidarity." Curiously, it too reassigns the subject positions in the frequent call of duty and obligation for solidarity: of whom it is asked, to whom it must be shown. Up until quite recently, it was the "young" who asked for it, demanded it, pleaded for it—marching, protesting, rebelling, striking (do we still remember "Global Strike Day" on March 15, 2019?) against the programmed "extinction" of their future. School children, too young to vote or take part in political life, left their classrooms all over the world pleading—in vain—that the future be saved. Their own future and that of the Earth, their future on this earth. They received nothing but platitudes, empty promises (in response to Greta's great speech at the UN of "How dare you": "the fantasy of economic growth"). Whether they know it or not, those revelers on beaches and in bars dancing in the summer night, ecstatic to have been liberated from confinement, laughing at the dangers of the virus, are only reversing the order of dependence—for life. And whether the generation complicit in bringing about or at least creating the conditions for this catastrophic collapse knows it or not, the virus, selectively targeting the old with a most cruel and difficult death, has reversed the order of solidarity, which the "young" now refuse to give.

(Of course, this reversal, this justice by revenge, will do nothing to repair the damage, still less to abolish the "wrong" (*tort*), in Lyotard's sense of the term: viruses will come and go, but the violence done to the Earth the young will inherit is to last forever or, at least, for hundreds of thousands of years.)

II (b)
Toronto, Fall / Winter, 2020

In the previous section I have asked: what world corresponds with this epidemic time as its other face and reverse side? This, however, is not exactly the right question. There is not one world, there is not one homogeneous, continuous time. There is an Outside.

The time of this epidemic is a time-zone, a Zone of time, embedded in, enveloped by other, world historical, geological, planetary . . . times.[35] The time that does not pass is itself not a passage of time; it does not succeed, follow, or come after another time, pushing it or letting it pass into the past, in accord with—following the order, law, and logic of—chronological time. An involution of time: closed upon itself, without exit. On the outside, we know (even if we are unable to think it, to convert this "knowledge" [*savoir*] into thought), times are rushing ahead just as before, out-spacing our capacity to think them, just as before. Signs burst through the semi-permeable envelope; news of "occurrences"—for they are not events—reach us from the outside: Siberia is burning, the ice sheet of Greenland has suffered an irreversible collapse; 70% of known living species have gone extinct; fierce fires, scorching heatwaves, ever more forceful hurricanes, invasions by locusts . . . traverse the terrain; on another plane, that of the World, the infrastructures holding up economies, socio-political structures, and cultural institutions—that is, our modern "civilization(s)"—are on the verge of "collapse," just as the eponymous new science has been predicting.

Unlike epidemic time, the times on the outside are prodigiously productive. Along different but interactive / interlacing / confluencing trajectories, they are rushing the World and the Planet ahead, toward disasters foretold long before this epidemic. ("L'effondrement total de notre planète, de la vie sur terre, vers le milieu du siècle prochain," René Dumont, 1974[36]). Space permits only to ask if this advance is still in what Blanchot called "historical time"? Of an infinitely open horizon, unending, even if passing from one disaster, from one catastrophe, one collapse (as collapsology argues) to another. Or, with the geocide on course, we have "departed from historical space"[37] and entered the new order of an ending (without end) of time.[38]

There is an Outside: what does this mean beyond the phenomenological description of our experiences that are structured by it? First, the Zone is not the Whole: impossible to flee, closed upon itself like a seashell, yet not the Whole (World). (Although it may appear that way on the inside, as all that remains of the World.) It is not *one*—uniform, homogeneous—world either, identical throughout with itself. (Although, again, this may be our experience on the inside). The inside is solicited, haunted from the Outside.

Without exit: in other words, without history, or *histoire*, narrative or witness testimony (one reason why analogies with the great epidemics of the past—historical or fictional, actual or mythical—break down and metaphors fail to do their work). "Epidemic literature" (Defoe's diaries or Thucydides' history, the fictions of Camus or Sophocles or Márquez) is a genre of the survivor, an actual or fictional narrator who remains outside and ahead of the story he tells. Bocaccio's *Decameron* is doubly a fiction: both the 100 tales and the young men and women who recount them as diversion from the grizzly story unfolding inside the walls of Florence, are Bocaccio's inventions, in the year of 1350, two years after the end of the plague. If to compose a narrative, to write a history or *histoire* is to forget (to do the work of mourning) or to create distance (*écarter*) by some other means (by offering up, for example, the "most fair and delightful planes" in 100 tales), the epidemic "here and now" does not let us forget. It leaves no space in between, permits no distance, not even the hairline of a gap, even less the fault line of an interval; it contaminates every space in between bodies, even the air that passes from mouth to mouth, even the non-space of the touch of touch. And the "in between," as noted before, is the condition of having or establishing or entering to a *relation*. Rare is therefore the discourse today that is truly contemporaneous, lets itself be marked by the time of this epidemic as its own time, while also evading the double danger Heidegger warned about: to posture either as diagnostic—discourse that is immune to the condition it stipulates as its own inescapable milieu (as in Agamben's prognostic provocations), or to become symptomatic (as is most mediatized / political discourse today), contaminated by fear, hysteria, and panic, whose denial (denegation) is only a different manifestation of the same contamination.

On the inside, we meander: search for virtual / provisory / hypothetical diagnoses of our condition; project / predict / forecast future scenarios, speculate about the world "after." "Where are we?" we ask. "Où suis-je,"[39] asks Bruno Latour in the first person. "Where have we landed?" and not, distancing ourselves from Latour this time, "where to land?" *Où atterrir?*[40] The time for such decisions is over. Are we traversing a crisis, a brutal but brief episode of an incursion? Are we *traversing* it, passing through it?—in which case, there will be an exit, an outcome, a world after to prepare and plan for, or even engineer. However far away it may be. Or are we at a turning point? A mutation, a change of epoch? In which case, according to Blanchot, we are already in the "world after." Indeed, did we not pass a point of turning without return some time ago? Is this global disaster, said to be the first, not a rehearsal for the great confinement (the climate catastrophe) yet to come and yet insidiously already at work everywhere? Or is it a repetition? The one disaster that reclaims *a posteriori* the epidemics of the past that at the time still appeared local and localized—the Ebola and Aids crises, the countless swine and bird flu epidemics, Zika, mad cow disease, SARS-1—as precursors? Reclaims them as preparations, as precursors announcing as unending and incalculable, at once predictable and yet unforeseeable, the cascade of catastrophes that characterizes this new epoch?

The truth is, we do not, we cannot, know. As Bataille writes inside another Zone, the war, in such a time "nothing can give [us] such knowledge."[41] And Blanchot's verdict regarding the inaccessibility of such knowledge is even more radical. Of knowing whether are at a turning point he writes:

> Si c'est une certitude, ce n'est pas un tournant. Le fait d'appartenir à ce moment où s'accomplit un changement d'époque (s'il y en a), s'empare aussi du savoir certain qui voudrait le déterminer, rendant inapproprié la certitude, comme l'incertitude.
>
> If it is a certainty, it is not a turning. The fact that one belongs to this moment where a change of epoch accomplishes itself also takes away the certain knowledge that would determine it, making certitude as inappropriate as incertitude.[42]

Or, Finding the World Again

The fact of turning itself places knowledge of it not just out of reach, but outside the region / register of (un)certainty. In which case, our not knowing where we are, where we have landed—in a crisis, which as always, will invent its exit (Deguy) or in a change of epoch whose turning is absolutely unknowable—is without repair. Our ignorance alone is certain, endemic to where we find ourselves, and will not serve as evidence for the one or the other scenario either way. Such is our situation inside the Zone. Such is the sense of the adjective in Jean-Luc Nancy's recent remark: "we have entered an epoch of *radical* uncertainty."[43]

What does this mean for thought, or, to borrow Jérôme Lèbre's title for his "chaîne" of reflections, for "philosophy in the time of the epidemic"? Silence? No, says Bataille. On the contrary, it is a rare "privilege to be in tune with the incompleteness of history."[44] This incursion or invasion (we do not yet know which) by the "thing" we have named Covid-19, this suspension of time's passage, is a chance to be contemporaneous with our time, to not arrive too late, after the flight of the Minerva. But this chance for timeliness is also an exigence, to not turn away but to hold onto (and these are the words of Bataille's contemporary, Blanchot) "the incompletion that it necessarily holds in it."[45]

Inside, we meander. On the outside, bugs and butterflies, the plants in my garden, birds on the trees, even domestic dogs . . . continue to live life as before, each according to its own rhythm, unique season, cycle of migration. Even better, some (many) flourish in our absence, reclaim (re-territorialize) the seas and the air, take over the urban spaces whence the virus has exiled us, forced us to evacuate. I watched a fox walk down on my street the other day. Untouched by the virus, immune / indifferent to / ignorant of the contagion, the micro motions of the plants on my balcony, the suddenly freed, unhindered circulation of other living creatures (whom we exiled to "nature" long ago), give a new sense to our separation. Their co-presence in what still appears to be the same space–time, the same air that we breathe, their proximity to our bodies, expose us to our own strange, newfound "Weltlosigkeit," our loss of the world, albeit not in the same fashion as the animal is said to be poor in world (*weltarm*) or plants (if their presence could be at all compared to rocks) are without world (*weltlos*), according to Heidegger.

Our separation is of a different order than one of inclusion / exclusion, of sharing or not sharing the same world or the world as such. It is categorical, and the line of separation (not of division) runs between World and Territory. Following this viral exposure / exhibition, it may appear that *we* are shut out of the same world that we shared before, when the same air was still passing between us. But the "territories" other living creatures territorialize, inhabit, cohabit, and inside whose boundaries they circulate so freely around my balcony, outside my home, in the city . . . are not continuous or commensurate with, do not communicate or compose or otherwise mix with what is "world." Of course, it may appear that all other living creatures claim a place in this world, but World and Territory are heterogeneous spaces. And while the latter is wholly outside the world, it does not constitute the Outside that from the outside haunts our lives inside the Zone of this epidemic.

Territories may overlap, coincide with, or be superimposed over the Zone, or, since they are mobile (flocks of birds, swarms of bees, continuously de- and re-territorialize), they may, like clouds, pass over the Zone without leaving a trace. But they do not compose with it (as musical notes in a composition reciprocally modify one another in a melody, or as images composing a montage give birth to something absolutely new). Territories do not conjugate or articulate with the Zone as its "other" face or reverse side, and which, haunting it from the Outside, would reciprocally define it as a Zone—of confinement, interdiction, or "other" space. It is not with regard to Territories that we should interrogate the Zone as neither the whole (World) nor as

Or, Finding the World Again

one (world) but as one element in a con-figuration, which, by way of hypothesis, I will consider here as a heterotopic structure, in the sense of Foucault's definition (invention) of the concept.[46]

A concept, staying still with the philosophical vocabulary of Deleuze, is at once a creation (of philosophy) and creative (productive of possible worlds). The concept "heterotopia" cuts up space differently and re-assembles the sites, emplacements, places it itself creates into a wholly other, dynamic configuration. It dramatizes the topos of the world and the world as topos. As Foucault's nomination implies, "Other" spaces are not passive containers of (active) objects and events; their alterity concerns not specific qualities but forces: the power to "suspect, neutralize, or invent" a set of relations. While irreducibly "other" and un-super-imposable, heterotopias impose on other sites—a relation, a con-figurations. In short, they are "agitators," contesting, soliciting, perverting, juxtaposing with . . . other sites in a network of rhizomatic relations in which they themselves are implicated.

Ordinary heterotopias (if such a term may apply to what is "other" by definition) are commonly dispersed throughout the fabric of the social world. Churches, cemeteries, airports, trains and train stations are among Foucault's "ordinary" examples. At the limit, the extreme case of "other spaces" is constituted by zones of interdiction: prisons, gulags, camps—refugee, labor and "re-education" camps; the "Jungle" in Calais, the camps holding the Uighurs in Xiang province, the whole island of Lesbos; insane asylums; spaces of internal and external exile (in the USSR, in the apartheid of South-Africa) . . . In a very different sense, the "America" of Günther Anders' exile during the war or the island of the shipwrecked Robinson (the other protagonist in Derrida's meditations on the loss of the world) also represent limit cases. Applying a certain "forcing" to Foucault's original concept, I will consider them as radical or "extreme heterotopias." (The Zone, as we will see, is doubly the extreme or limit case—of heterotopic *spaces* and of the *concept* of

On the Absence of the World, One More Time

heterotopia itself: it touches the limit in / of space, it carries alterity to the very limit of its possibility, the possibility of pertaining to the category of "space"; and there, at the point where "alterity" could not be further radicalized, it brings the concept to the limit of its [im]possibility.)

Is the Zone an Other space?

The three examples below may pave the way to an answer by permitting a closer examination of the "extremity" of both the space and the concept.

> *Through the dense wire mesh on the window of her cell, the prisoner watches someone enter a building across the street. The man probably pays no attention to it but, on her side of the world, which is a world, this effortless passage through a door on the other side is in the order of a "miracle." The exception on which order rests on the inside and which reciprocally defines the street as its Outside.*

> *The camera slowly "travels" along the barbed-wire fence of the abandoned camp. Across the fence, it films an ordinary open field. The silhouette of a church tower punctuating the horizon in a distance suggests the presence a village: "another planet" says the narrator (Night and Fog /* Nuit et Brouillard[47]*)—at once infinitely close-by and at an infinite distance.*

> *A group of armed Chechens take over the crowded Dubrovka Theater during a performance in Moscow. Some hostages are killed during the siege and up to 204 die in a botched rescue attempt. When after 83 hours of captivity a survivor finds herself alone on the street, the cafes are full, the street is crowded with pedestrians, cars and buses are running as before. In all that time—an "enfer" of time inside the theater, its density, its contraction, immeasurable by chronometry—time on the outside has continued to pass, measurably (83 hours) just as before.*

Or, Finding the World Again

The first question to ask: what or whose passage is interdicted—by law, geography, the force of arms, or by the virus? Whose passage from inside a "zone" is blocked to an outside and vice versa? For subjects, bodies—dead or alive—will pass, even if in a controlled and regulated manner. Guards will pass, daily; the same holds for supplies and deliveries (a surreptitious route of escape, as we know from one of the best informants, the cinema). The prisoner, the inmate, will be or may be eventually released or liberated. What, however, cannot pass over this wall, actual or virtual, what cannot circulate on both sides of the interval, is sense, while still making sense, while making the same sense. The space of confinement is absolutely heterogeneous with what lies outside, its Outside, with regard to "sense." The sense the two worlds as worlds that *make* sense make—especially when it concerns the loss of sense or world; when, as we know from the witness, Primo Levi, the sense that makes "world" and the sense that the world makes is "nonsense." It is not that nothing makes sense, but that the absence of sense ("Hier ist kein warum"[48]) alone makes sense and is the sense that the world—or indeed, the universe, for it is a wholly other space, *l'univers concentrationnair*—fabricates daily, with every (senseless) blow.

A correlate still of this first question regards the "sense" (of confinement) confined to the Zone of this epidemic: to what other space, to what outside, can it not pass, while still being solicited, doubly, by a sense of "elsewhere"? The sense that this confined sense is productive of an "elsewhere" and that this elsewhere is no more than a (mere) sense. Once the epidemic becomes a pandemic, englobing everything, the outside, its other face and reverse side, is not only inaccessible; it becomes a space, as space, geographically unlocalizable. Not a utopia, for while it is nowhere, it means not that it is not anywhere else or is not an "elsewhere," an *ailleurs*.

I have been watching cinema from pre-epidemic times, that is to say, from the history of the cinema: everything extracted from this world—touch, face, crowd—is there. Effortlessly, naturally, unselfconsciously. The very possibility of their absence is in the region of the unthought / unthinkable, the unthinkable unthought. And yet, this cinematic space—whether represented, or projected, or the cinema's own space in the theatre—does not articulate or compose with the world "here and now" to reciprocally define it as a Zone.

This cinema is of the past, today gone, *parti*, absent. More precisely, its world is past, the world in which it still claimed a place on earth ("une place sur la terre," is how Godard names his cinema) is gone and will not return— not even as Godard prays, "in the time of the resurrection" ("l'image viendra au temps de la résurrection"[49]). This cinema certainly merits a backward glance (of the kind that Lot's wife cast back at the "empty windows of the tall house," "the courtyard where [she] sang," in the magnificent short poem of Akhmatova[50]), even if by such "last regard" we risk becoming paralysed, like Lot's wife, who has no name, by nostalgia. Still, it is not the past, it is not past cinema, the past / memory of the cinema, or the past archived and projected by the cinema that haunts life inside the Zone from the Outside. And we can say this with some measure of confidence, even if we do not (yet) know how to say / how to think what that Outside is.

The one other significant distinguishing feature of radical heterotopias is reversibility. Inside the juxtaposition, the direction of solicitation gets reversed. In "ordinary" heterotopias (church, theatre, cemetery) the articulation of spaces is relatively stable. As structures, they resist the solicitation / contestation (of the "hetero") at work on the interior of the articulation itself. Radical heterotopias, on the other hand, easily destabilize. The direction of forces active on the interior of the con-figuration gets reversed, the relation of the disjunction, topos / heterotopos, pivots, and the quality of being "other," the force of alterity, gets transferred to the other side of the interval. (Silently, invisibly, such a transfer has already taken place here

Or, Finding the World Again

in this text. We can already see that it is the hetero-topos in the Foucauldian schema, the Zone inside in which we live, that is being contested; that the "Other" space in the configuration is the Outside, even though we cannot yet say what sort of space it is.)

The prisoner will be eventually liberated; the same holds for the hostages who do not die in the attack; the camp will be rendered inoperative, its ruins preserved, not as a memorial, but as testimony to the unthinkable. The theatre will return to being the same heterotopia it has always been—an "other" space for staging fictional other spaces. But when the prisoner looks back from the street outside at her window covered with wire mash, what she will see is an opening to a wholly other world on the other side (of her "this" side). Tourists, but also former inmates visiting the ruins of the camp, will have to summon all the powers of imagination to project the radical alterity of an other continent onto the meadow or the church tower on the other side of the fence. As for the liberated hostage, by the time the world on the busy Moscow street at night has tilted upright again, the terror, so cruelly and absolutely real just a few minutes ago, will have begun to sink into the irreality of a nightmare.

A second, albeit provisional question arises at this point: will the abyssal hiatus that has opened up in the fabric / tissue of the world here and now close up just as spontaneously as it has appeared, leaving behind nothing but an ugly scar? In memory of the massive humiliation visited upon the World, the absurdity of compulsive hand washing, of distancing from every other as Other? Will the world turn upright again, will time slip back to its joint and begin to turn again? Or, should one rather say, give oneself trouble here by pointing out that the memory of the absurd, of the past as absurd, is a forgetting; whereas a scar, as Deleuze writes, citing the Stoics, "is not the sign of a *past* wound but of 'the *present* fact of having been wounded'"?[51] In which case, the world after, should there be one, is / will itself be a world scarred. (The other day, I watched an opera telecast form the Scala of Milan: except for the fictional characters on the stage, everyone, the conductor, Riccardo Chailly, members of the orchestra, and the entire audience, was masked. On one side of the proscenium, the world that was, the word as was, appears as fiction in a heterotopic space; watching it from the other side of an invisible line, in real space, spectators appear to mourn the passing of that same world, its *disparition,* in Japanese style, by uniformly wearing white masks.) The scar is not made of the same substance as the world, it will not seamlessly rejoin only cover over—mask— the cut of the interval dividing the two sides.

There are two complementary responses to these concerns.

The first pertains to time or, better yet, to space–time. For one could easily see that this transference (approximating the psychoanalytic sense of the term) of the alterity from one to the other side of the interval is facilitated, or indeed, is conditional on a corresponding, simultaneously operative heterochronia. A schism also opens in time and it will not be healed by a scar. There will be no synthesis in the place of the scar. Time itself pivots along the axis cut between inside / outside; it splits into two heterogeneous, discontinuous temporalities. The two "continents" of sense will not be held together in time, in the same order of time. So when Primo Levi passes what he calls his "chemical exam" inside the camp, he has the definite sensation "of not being believed, of not even believing it himself," that in 1941 in Turin he took his degree in chemistry;[52] and later on, while sitting at a table and writing this very testimony (*Survival in Auschwitz*), he himself is not quite convinced that what he is writing about actually happened.[53] And when Günther Anders returns to Paris from his exile in America after the war—a jubilant return: "Paris est là!"—the many years spent on the other side quickly recede into oblivion. From this side of the other side, he has the greatest difficulty in pronouncing "our telephone number over there (*là bas*)"; or the number of a cousin in New York who (as he imagines) "in this moment is sitting in front of his typewriter, trying to evoke the Europe that is absent, while we over here . . . are traversing the forbidden landscapes of old times."[54]

Again, the two "continents" will not be held together in time, in the same order of time.

(The "other side of this side": the "sides" are reversible; "otherness" oscillates, moves from one to the other side of the interval, the operator of alterity that heterogenizes the two spaces. This means not that alterity is relative [no longer irreducible], only that in the case of radical heterotopias, the "world" is no longer a measure, is no longer there to be the measure.)

The second response to the questions posed above, and which also takes the form of questions, concerns the Outside: whence the solicitation, the contestation of life inside the Zone—restless, nervous, exhausted, and irritated? How is the (com)pulsion to flee—to go somewhere, to be anywhere else, outside the Zone—permanently frustrated, while also simultaneously maintained? Since the epidemic has become a pandemic, since it has reterritorialized the entire globe, leaving us no space to flee, what other space remains to reciprocally define what is now the whole world, the Zone, as not the Whole? We appear to live (in) the extraordinary situation that there is nowhere outside the Zone; in other words, it is the Nowhere that defines the whole world as a Zone and thus not the Whole.

When "elsewhere" is not somewhere else, when it is not an "anywhere" somewhere else, it is nowhere. It is the Nowhere. (And what other space could be more deserving of the title, "Other"?)

Kafka's old parable, "The Departure," may cast light upon our predicament: The "master" saddles his horse and goes to the gate. When his servant asks where he is going, he replies: out of here, anywhere.[55] Our desire to flee, to exit from this Zone to anywhere, is no less impatient and could not be any stronger.

But the virus, which is everywhere, leaves us no other space, no other space than Nowhere.

That the Outside is Nowhere is not a negative proposition. On the contrary, it posits, names the limit case: the Outside is the limit case. Not a no-place, utopia or fiction, or an imaginary space, but a zero-degree space, the zero-degree case of the space and of the concept of heterotopia. The Outside *is* Nowhere. The limit case of heterotopia, it is the skin of the world. It takes up no space, it is the limit-line, the lining of the limit. It is as such limitrophic space that it carries the concept of heterotopia itself to its limit: the limit of its (im)possibility, where it deconstitutes itself.

III
Toronto, Winter, 2020 / Spring 2021

During a solitary visit to the park bench where I habitually draft my notes for this text, a blue surgical mask slips out from between the pages of my diary. The *unheimlich* encounter with this by now ubiquitous object in this unexpected place sets off another enigmatic event. A "puresprungforth," to borrow once again Celan's borrowing of Hölderlin's "entspungenes," a "pur jailli," in Lacoue-Labarthe's French translation. It instantaneously intervenes in my troubled reflections on the timeliness (contemporaneity) of Celan's "sentence" regarding the fate of world "here and now." Rare are such felicitous occurrences (as Derrida also noted): something, a word or an image arrives from an elsewhere (*d'ailleurs*) and, as if by the turn of a kaleidoscope, without changing or adding anything, any new element, it instantaneously transforms everything. This time, it is a thought, or an "ideational content" as Freud says (in *Civilization and its Discontents*) of another pure intuition: "the world is gone" refers to the "here and now." It concerns "here and now": it is the world "here and now" that is departing, leaving, absenting itself; "here and now" is a world voiding / emptying itself of what constitutes it, of what makes it "world."

As noted before, Derrida does not ask about the world: what, which, or whose world is gone, absent, or lost. Celan's? Or Heidegger's "world as such" that is the guiding thread of the last seminar? Or is it Derrida's own? The world we could still share with him as a world in common, whose future we still had in common at the time of the seminar? But not after the turn or rupture in the order of time indexed here by a date in the common calendar, 2019? Instead of asking about the world, Derrida turns to the state and condition designated by the adjectival form of the past participles in several languages, *fort, parti,* gone; he develops, invents, donates . . . in the course of the seminar a vertiginous series of "interpretations" of the German participle "fort": (*le monde*) *est parti, s'en est allé, est loin, est perdu, il n'y a plus de monde* (31–2); "un non-monde qui n'est pas immonde" (32); "nous sommes *weltlos*, nous sommes sans monde"; the world is absent, it distances itself: "le fait indéniable qu'il n'y a pas de monde, pas même un monde, pas même un seul et même monde, pas de monde un: *le* monde, *un* monde, un monde *un*, c'est ce qu'il n'y a pas . . . " (367). I've placed the "world," "le" or "un monde," in between parentheses so as to indicate that in these metonymic chains of interpretations and improvisations the "world" is an invariable constant, neither implicated nor caught up in the play of the variations of absence set free by the past participle "fort."

There are several reasons for Derrida's "negligence," his avoidance of naming any particular world. Two are relevant here. First, the target of his deconstructions, as always in the later period, is the concept, be it "world" or "hospitality," "gift" or "time"; the aim of deconstruction is to carry the concept to its absolute limit, to the limit of its (im)possibilty, the point of its auto-deconstruction. (In the seminar, this point arrives when death finally neutralizes the force—*Walten*—that reigns everywhere in the living world.) The second reason explains the first:

On the Absence of the World, One More Time

in the time, in the still historical space of the seminar (2003 in calendar time), the ground (*sol, terre, fond*, foundation) holding up the world (of deconstruction and of the seminar itself) has not yet moved; the menace, the threat of the in-existence (not the absence or departure or loss) of the world of Da-sein, the ground of its being-there, into which Da-sein is thrown (and out of which, as Freud says, the fully narcissistic ego cannot believe it could fall), does not yet define or defy the horizon of the thinkable, of what is thinkable by deconstruction.

Today, in the here and now of this epidemic time, the substantive and the participle, the "world" and its predicated state—"gone," "lost," etc.—are inexorably linked. They cannot be thought separately or sequentially. The loss of the world here and now is an intensely experienced acuity, an inescapable, palpable actuality. It is the unmediated concretum of the "here and now." It is *the* "here and now." (For this reason, it cannot be metaphorized; analogies cannot be drawn with the great epidemics of the past or the great confinement described by Foucault, or with the viral threat and fear of "terrorism." It is an interiority without separation, distance, or interval—or, as we said, the elsewhere is nowhere.)

Gone, absent, departed . . . is not another world. Not "your" world alone, nor the world "you" and "I" still had in common and which now (here and now) is lost, so that I must carry "you"—either to "here," to this world, or carry "you" within me, but still to the "here and now" of my annunciation—a place on earth, even if not in a world. In fact, the world "here and now" is not lost, gone, passed, in the past, to be mourned, commemorated, fictionalized, and beyond reach. It is not even a world of which we could still say with Derrida who cites Heidegger that it does not "world" (*weltet*) anymore. For there is production, a constant negative production. The "here and now" is a location in the world where the world unmakes and absents itself, decomposes and deconstitutes itself; where its tissue is being unraveled. Traces of this negative labor, neither destruction nor

Or, Finding the World Again

deconstruction, are everywhere: "closed," "for rent," "for lease"—signs of businesses departed; the last film title still on the billboard of the local theatre; empty paper boxes on the sidewalk; chairs in strict formation piled up on the table tops of deserted cafes; buses and street cars running past without passengers; cars parked on the same spot for weeks; theaters, museums, libraries—neither institutions nor heterotopias, only empty buildings. But these traces, marking the presence of this or that absence, are secondary surface effects; they are symptomatic of a profound operation in the course of which the immaterial substance of which the fabric of the world is made and incessantly remade is being relentlessly extracted. I will discuss here only two sets of composite "elements" (I am missing a word here as they are not building blocks): the face and the gaze, and the touch and the interval, which, in their infinitely rich *agencements* (not inter-actions), are world-creating, productive of local, localized, and ephemeral micro-worlds.

Face / Gaze

Faces, rather than the face. Faces in the plural, as in Cassavetes' eponymous cinema, register / transmit / translate / transform / project / repress / amplify / reflect / betray . . . the invisible they alone make visible. Forces, desires, fears, terrors, passions . . . traverse their surface, set off vibrations, produce resonances in between, which then compose the "live" music (sonata, chamber music, rhapsody, or fugue . . .) that the close-up of the cinema is especially suited to amplify and play back in its own cinematic time. Bataille writes the "tears of eros," Barthes devotes a short text to the face of Garbo,[56] and, in the film *Manhattan*, Woody Allen names the smile, not of Mona Lisa, but of "Tracy" (Margo Hemingway) among the ten things worth living for. In contrast, *the* face is an abstraction: Levinas' or Lacan's face looms up on the horizon; it awaits me, commands me, virtually solicits me, precedes me, waiting for me, "there," even before I will have arrived. Deleuze's face is yet another apparatus of capture: of subjectivation. The abstraction need not even materialize as a face, it may appear in effigy, the *sound* of footsteps, a *blind* window; the close-up image (Deleuze) of anything will suffice to "impersonate" the apparatus, activate its power to command, to survey, to hold me captive.

The face of Garbo may be a marble face, a snow-covered arctic landscape, in other words a pure mask, and yet, it is singularly Garbo's face and no one else's: inimitable, non-appropriable, and yet not a property. Not even a "self." At the other pole or end of the spectrum "faces": the face(s) of Duras, "scorched by deep dry wrinkles, the skin is cracked . . . I have a face laid waste," an active landscape and a time code, an individuated site without a subject. "It has been my face,"[57] she writes, looking at the photograph of an old face, now shed as skin is shed. In the world, the face is exposed to the "weather" of the world (as Anselm Kiefer's paintings are exposed to climatic changes outside his studio). Things arrive / happen to it from both sides. The inside and the outside. After thirty, Camus said somewhere, you are responsible for your face. Perhaps not every face is unlike any other. But to *have* a face is to have the only one ever, until forever, in the universe. And this is not a question of beauty but of individuation, the effacement, precisely, of a generic face.

The face is not a screen (that hides) but a membrane (that shows). Think of Giacometti's face: a sensible surface that marks / is marked by time, age, passions passing across it ("worn out by desire" writes Duras of the lover's face[58]); it is a membrane with memory, it archives traces of tremors, terrors, vibrations, and waves—of fatigue, shame, desire, anger, horror, embarrassment, hesitation, joy—and finally, the rigid, absolutely unique silence of death.

"All humanity wears or has worn a mask," even before entering history, writes Roger Caillois.[59] "All of ethnology is filled with masks, and with the vertigo, the trances, the hypnoses, and the panics that are its nearly inevitable conse-

Or, Finding the World Again

quences." Caillois calls it a "second face," emphasizing that the mask—of rituals, festivals, religious or war ceremonies, carnivals, etc., in particular the kind we find displayed in ethnographic museums—does not hide, conceal, or even screen a face. In fact, it is more than a face, more than any face. The mask does not just transform the idea of the face, it abolishes it, something else appears in its place (on the front of the head, where the face should be) and something happens in this place—there appears a new category of an object in the world, an *über-gesicht*, a *sur-visage*, a sight / site of becoming: becoming Other, the divine, the dead, or the totem animal, at once intimidating, seductive, powerful, dangerous—the bearer of death. The mask of the Medusa (the title of one of Caillois' books) is perhaps the meta-sign, the master signifier of all masks.

The masks, ubiquitous today—surgical, medical, or homemade, uniformly covering, by law, every face in public spaces, on the street, in elevators, on the metro—serve a necessary utilitarian function, not unlike an umbrella against the rain. But on another, discontinuous plane, they have a radically different performative effect. ICU doctors compensate for it by wearing a photograph of their face over their chest, at eye level with the patient's face. For they know that their mask is privative, that it de-faces. (Not unlike the destructive work of the iconoclasts of the Protestant Reformation, during the "beeldenstorm" in the lowlands of Northern Europe. The retable in the Jan van Arkel Chapel in the Domkerk of Utrecht, showing five figures seated around the throne of the Virgin, all uniformly defaced by a large white plaster stain, uncannily composes a montage with the common group portraits of public figures seated around conference tables, all masked.)

Privation is not creative. It does not transform the face into a "head" (of Bacon) or into a body part, a block of flesh (of Deleuze). It renders "you," facing me, as it were, without "wearing" your face—not anonymous. This is not the right word here, it is not "your" name that is missing here. Still, something is missing, from the world. Not by virtue of a "veiling effect," well known to painters ever since Parrhaisios painted the perfect veil, a "teaser," as it would be called today, to incite the desire to unveil. No such desire is implanted by "your" mask, which, defacing you, extracts something from the world. This something, paradoxically, is my own visibility. The presence of your face in the world (in the fullest sense of the word "face") is the condition of I myself becoming visible, of making an appearance not just in but for the world.

"Larvatus prodeo," masked I move forward, announces Descartes, inventing the "conceptual personage" of the philosopher as the spectator of the theatre of world, who, in the mathematical point it occupies, is not present to / does not present itself to the world. The world, separate (*écarté*) on the other side of an interval, is a blind spectacle, a dead object that does not look back. Such is the condition of its "objectivity." By virtue of an analogous logic, the mask that defaces you turns me into another blind object that cannot look back at you, recognize you as the cohabitant of this same world. At the same time, my own face-covering separates me, cuts me off from the world to which I am now not present, cannot present myself, and which is a world (but does it still merit the name "world"?) that has only spectators, atomized, solitary subjects: dispersed, meandering in neutral, disconnected spaces, passing / evading one another. A non-world ("un non-monde qui n'est pas immonde") without encounters.

Together with the face, the mask extracts from the tissue of the world the rich, effervescent, fleeting events that take place on and in between faces. For the mask is not a surface or a screen. It is nothing, dead space. It swallows up what one may call "face-events" in the world: storms of rage, waves of laughter, smiles like Jeanne Moreau's, the jouissance Lacan told us was known to Bernini's Saint Theresa; it blots out the gaze (eyes become two black holes that may look at me but do not see me); it also obliterates from the world the mouth, this hole in the middle,

Or, Finding the World Again

the sight and site of (Bacon's) scream, the opening whence enters the world Lulu's cry, the throat singer's song, both terrible, yet sheltering an existence in crisis (Deleuze), and, though it is rarely masked, the tiny rounded "o" of a hole that releases like soap bubbles Donald Trump's chain of lies . . . It also wipes out the mouth that is tight-lipped or foul-mouthed, the smile that betrays a lie or fakes joy, or when it curls up in a cry or, scorn, is depressed, irritated, contemptuous, in despair.

Proximity / Distance: Touch and the Crowd

Everything or almost everything[60] that could be said of Touch (*le toucher*) was said by Derrida touching (rather than touching on: what a difference this small word makes!) the corpus of Jean-Luc Nancy.[61] It would be futile (impossible) to summarize or paraphrase or otherwise try to supplement this text. Instead, I will try to bring into relation two otherwise distant concepts: Touch and Crowd. Both are the affairs of the body, both are modulators of distance and proximity. It is as such that, together, they make and remake the social body, exhibit and put on display the world as a vibrating tissue of relations, sensible passages, connections, communications . . .

True, Touch marks the limit of all possible con-tact; it is the lining or the membrane in common that cannot be appropriated and cannot not be shared. It "exists" only as sharing in between. Still, the famous interdiction "noli me tangere" (I discuss it elsewhere in reference to Fra Angelico's painting and its interpretation by Didi-Huberman[62]) is a beautiful example of how delicate and subtle, yet powerful, touch can be from a distance. In Fra Angelico's painting as I recall, the line of the force of touch is not represented (as this would be intrusive and destroy the delicacy of the painting's touch). It is only hinted at by a few red spots, blood stains or rose petals running / floating between the body of Mary Magdalene and the just resurrected Christ. There is proximity, intimacy in this carefully calibrated distance. From too far, nothing passes in between; too close or too fast (for touch is also movement), the touch becomes intrusive, violent (nowadays it would be called, called out as harassment).

Crowds on the other hand are themselves bodies (without organs): plastic, malleable, self-forming, self-reforming, self-deforming. They absorb you and release you, receive you and let you go. They are composed of particle-bodies (not unlike the famous frontispiece image of Hobbes' *Leviathan*): backs and fronts, or profiles, mostly heads; occasionally a face emerges for a fleeting moment, the likes of which Baudelaire (himself a man of the crowd) celebrates.

Crowd-bodies are also a-subjective / impersonal *operators* of bodies: their distance and proximity, their elastic, flexible distribution in space, their formation in synchronized movement. Like gases, crowds occupy available spaces and, accordingly, contract and densify or expand and relax, as if a living organism, an octopus on the sea bed changing shape, or a flock of birds flying in formation, moving together.

Crowds are also an affair of the cinema, which, among all the arts, is best suited to compose its own movements with their "kinesis." The opening scene, so familiar from (good and bad) cinema, gives the crowd as the living organism it is: bodies spill out from crowded carriages into the morning light of the platform, then past the narrow doors, spilling out onto the avenue, they join the flow already in movement, heads rhythmically bobbing up and down, until the camera finds what it is looking for. A face. For crowds are neither faceless nor mute. They are filled with faces, and thoughts: in Wim Wenders' cinema (*Himmel über Berlin*) angels (the camera) descend from the sky to hear those thoughts, while Baudelaire's man of the crowd absorbs them through the window of a café:

> . . . a convalescent is enjoying the sight of the passing crowd, identifying himself in thought with all the thoughts that are

Or, Finding the World Again

moving around him . . . he breathes in with delight all the spoors and odors of life . . . In the end he rushes out into the crowd in search of a man unknown to him whose face, which he had caught sight of, had in a flash fascinated him.[63]

Faces, crowds, bodies in their variable, forever fluctuating, mutating, changing degrees of contact, in their spontaneous yet calibrated display of distance and proximity, composing a confluence one may plunge into as if a benevolent river—such is the stuff of which the world is made or of which it makes and incessantly remakes itself. And such is our absolutely exceptional situation today, here and now, that this "stuff" is no longer here, *and* that this "no longer" is irreducible a) to familiar forms of absence: gone, departed, lost or absent here, only to be present elsewhere, in memory, in literature, in the cinema (these representations cannot but be deceptive should they imply that such a loss or departure will be compensated by the arts or the art of memory); or b) to what Celan and Derrida, Derrida's Celan, may have meant by "the *world* is gone." All this leaves us with the task of thinking, of trying to say with some degree of precision, what new sense this "sentence" (judgement) of Celan may have just acquired, what new form of a relation to the world this "no longer" signifies.

The "tissue of the world": I am not turning to this familiar idiom as figure or metaphor, both referential, but turn it instead into a concept productive of a possible world. Composed of / composing itself as a tissue, it is held up as scaffold by the skeletal structure immanent to it: points (of contact) and lines (of communication, transference, transmission, contraction).

The con-tact is between bodies: it is the face-to-face, confrontation, touch (caress, kiss, or just a punch, or even a gaze that is touching). Points are where bodies contact, in passion contract or are held together in the beehive of crowds. The lines, on the other hand, both link and separate, at once separate and conjoin the points (bodies) they themselves distribute in space, in mobile webs, in mutating matrices of contacts. In one dimension (transversally), the lines cut intervals that rhythmically structure and heterogenize space, are creative of ("other") spaces. To borrow once again from Heidegger, the line "spaces." In the other dimension (of longitude), the same lines redouble as open paths of communication, transmit signs, signals, missives, forces and passions, cries and whispers . . . and the virus. The world, however, is not the Tissue, but a tissue-effect—of spacing, the play of distance and proximity, intimacy and separation. It takes place (as Hannah Arendt said, even in dark times) in between.[64] Its event takes place in the gaps, in the hollow of the in between; the world is the event of it taking place in the interstices that lie in between. Therein lies its inherent fragility.

There are three discrete registers in which such a world may be undone, overturned, perverted, or turned against itself: the political, the conceptual, and the viral.

i.

In the order of the political, tyrannies, dictatorships, totalitarian and other regimes of violence and terror target precisely the Tissue: the major and minor, formal and informal, public and intimate, collective and private networks that hold a world together as World; or rather, since the Tissue as structure does not give itself birth, will not renew or repair itself, the target of repressive machinery is the "operator" of the Tissue, the *agencement* responsible for its spontaneous (re)production, creation, invention; in other words, a world that worlds itself. This is why the target of totalizing regimes (as the name already implies) is always a whole world, never part of it.

Pure violence (Idlib, Monrovia, Chad, the Rohingya, Yemen, ISIS, the Lord's Resistance Army, or Boko Haram are emblems

Or, Finding the World Again

standing in for a forever growing and mutating incomplete list) tears the Tissue apart, which turns into the generator of a generalized dis-order. Turmoil or "tumultus" is active, as a volcano whose irruptions are incalculable and unpredictable is active. Yet, paradoxically, it is also paralyzed in the face of the impetus of its own violence, which it cannot resist, in which it cannot intervene or find an exit from. (In this ambivalence, active / passive, the state may resemble Agamben's notion of "stasis," but the concept of civil war, whose violence is at once political and familiar, pertains to another possible world, other than Tissue. It is founded on a single cut and fundamental division: polis / oikos.[65]) The spectacle of pure terror (marauding militias, suicide bombs, random massacres, public executions and mutilations . . .) installs fear in the hearts, which, like the virus, penetrates every con-tact, infects, corrupts, perverts every link and contaminates every space, precisely in between. It is there that a world takes place as non-world, where it is being lost, is departing in the continuous present.

State (sponsored) violence (Stalin's USSR, Assad's Syria, the Taliban, the fascist regimes of Latin America, the Khmer Rouge, even the Cultural Revolution whose purges took place with complicity of the state) wages an organized, calculated, targeted—total or selective—war on the Tissue: on its lines of communications, points of con-tact, and above all, the intervals. For the latter heterogenize / pluralize / differentiate (and shelter the difference of) spaces, orders, classes, hierarchies; they insert the "wall" (the law of the Greeks) between the polis and the oikos, public and private, the home and the street, work and play, art (fiction) and the real, virtual and actual, city and the country, urban and rural . . . The Khmer Rouge of Cambodia touched the limit of the absolute (complete) destruction of the Tissue as such, on whose ruins, on the ruins of the World as Tissue, it imposed by the force of a terrible violence a wasteland. Literally and figuratively, a homogenized plane of faceless, undifferentiated mass uniformity, without memory or history.

On the Absence of the World, One More Time

(Heterogeneity, which is productive, is dangerously incalculable. Hence all totalitarianism is a variant of uniformity; hence its penchant for uniforms: Mao suits, MAGA hats, clichés for ideas and preformatted discourses. Even peoples must be uniform[ed]: the Uighurs either disappear or become Hun Chinese.)

Recent history provides two other variants of total domination over the Tissue as world-making. The one interferes with ("parasites" in the French sense of this ambivalent term, as static, as noise "parasites" signals of communication) the Tissue from the outside; the other, parasitically (now in the sense of the common English word) grafts itself onto its networks from the inside. (I defer here to Michel Serres' extraordinary work on the ambiguity inherent in the figure and the relation that is the Parasite.[66]) The first model, whether an intensification, totalization, or hyperbolization of Foucault's "gentle" method of "surveiller et punir," superimposes on the existing web of the World / the web that worlds its unique system of panopticon. Power flows in one direction, from a single centralized point or perspective, to atomized subjects it itself distributes in an homogenized and policed space. Here the Chinese undertaking that today digitally "disciplines (surveys) and punishes" total populations (schools, factories, neighborhoods, entire cities, ethnic groups) stands out as at once exemplary and an exception. It is a mutation, indeed a "mutant," of the old apparatus of Bentham. A digital infrastructure of brand-new networks, platforms, gateways, clouds, codes, algorithms, applications, etc., effectuates a wholly other, not only virtual but digital world. It is a world no longer analogous with and, therefore, cannot be translated back to the "real" from which it is fully detached. Its augmented machine vision, automated sensing machines, tracking systems, and smart (mobile) helmets with 360 degree vision ... not only make the world transparent and visible beyond any human perception, but also only machine readable. The machine (artificial intelligence), omnipresent in

Or, Finding the World Again

actual and virtual (cyber) space, observes, codes and decodes, remembers and recalls, every instant, storing and creating personal histories and collecting "big data" . . . (As it also punishes with great precision, it eliminates the element of hazard—of the "if and when" justice strikes, which Benjamin considered essential to the force of the law.) The Tissue that worlds—the play of distance and proximity, of the intimacy of the face-to-face, the pleasures of momentary / anonymous invisibility in a mobile crowd . . . —is not dismantled. It is ruined, overlaid, as if by molasses, by a monstrous digital tissue. The latter in fact is a wholly other world, neither habitable, nor sensible (in every sense of this word), or livable. For human perception or experience, it is entirely inaccessible.[67]

A well-known example of the second variant (which traces its origin at least as far back as the eighteenth century, to Metternich's network of spies) is the system of surveillance perfected by the STASI of East Germany. It penetrates the Tissue in depth. Secretively (but not secretly, for the existence of the system is / needs to be public knowledge if it is to have force), it takes up residence on the interior, insinuates itself at its most intimate points, most private networks. Here the analogy with parasitism lies with pathogenic biological agents, such as the virus, which for its very life must appropriate, "vampirize," the life-creating and life-sustaining machinery of the host. The surveillance of the life-creating connective Tissue of a community, of its network of communications productive of a world, itself becomes a network. An alien tissue grafted onto the first, active on its interior, it converts friends, enemies, and strangers, lovers and brothers . . . into its own agents, informants, captives of another Tissue, that is, another world, which it itself worlds. This other world, while not parallel with the first, saps its life, fatally weakens its powers to world.

Whether applied in pure form or in different combinations, the above modalities are counter-productions. Unlike revolutions, which, as Hannah Arendt says, inescapably confront us with the problem of beginning, they are reactive, reductive rarefactions. Still, they are incessantly at work; for the undoing of the World cannot cease and must be vigilantly performed without interruptions. It must go on without pause or rest, for the *World* will not / cannot cease "to world." (Hence the necessary paranoia / vigilance of all such regimes.)

ii.

On the plane of concepts (philosophy), movement is in the opposite direction: toward flows, the liberation of forces, intensities, and becomings, that is, a world creative of its own events, immanently engendering itself. Forces of (organic / inorganic) life come to traverse the grid, agitate the Tissue, send ripples through it, giving birth to world(s) that will not correspond with any familiar idea or the term "world." Such a birth is not an affair of representation or reference. It takes place on the conceptual plane (where the Tissue itself is situated) and is the performative of a concept that acts into, brings the Tissue—not to the point of destruction or devastation, as does tyranny—but to the cusp of mutation, to a point where the Tissue pivots from structure to fields—of forces, speeds, intensities, affects.

The singular cases of Bataille and of Deleuze (irreducibly discrete and yet in their philosophical sensibility exhibiting a proximity that is often overlooked) stand out as exemplary in this regard.

Bataille's concept of *intimacy*[68] (immanence, flow, "like water in water") dissolves the point (discrete, separate) and "sacrifices" the subject, as distinct, discrete, and atomized, a "thing" in a world of things, a "punctual" presence (da-sein) on which the Tissue, the world as tissue, is predicated. "Sacrifice" is at once conceptual and actual. The act on the plane of the mythical-shamanistic ritual (which Bataille planned to perform[69]) is repeated on the conceptual plane by the *concept* "sacrifice" as the destruction of the "thing" that everything, including the subject, necessarily is in the discontinuous sphere (of things). In sacrifice (the practice *and* the concept) the "subject" is returned to its proper immanence, to the intimate domain. In the ecstasy of eroticism, the atomized, zipped up "individual" is torn open; the separate, distinct being is opened up to "intimacy": to waves of anguish, spasms of tears and laughter, to the thunderbolt of ecstasy passing through it. By consequence, the *point* of con-tact (the space in-between) also dissolves: in the ecstasy of a deep kiss, the "distinction between our lips is lost"; in the communication of "two overlapping lacerations," which possesses a value the terms did not have, all other values, all other terms, are annihilated.[70]

If in the theatre of Bataille (who "rather than eat prefer[s] to be eaten"[71]), "intimacy" is the vanishing point where the subject returns to immanence, enters into communication like water in water, or wound upon wound, the philosophy of Deleuze sets the rigid grid itself into motion, gives it its proper time, in other words, inscribes it in a temporal register.[72] On the plane of Deleuzian cartography, the point becomes a "block of duration," con-tact mutates into "encounter," to a "becoming" that is a becoming other, a wholly other (being) irreducible to its constituent parts. The line is not anonymous or a-personal, nor a neutral element in a globally given preexisting structure. If it carries a name, it pertains to the singularity of a subject, or since the term "subject" no longer applies, to a processus of individuation. The line, as the limit or the outside, is the "means" of individuation. It links Captain Ahab (of Melville) directly to the white whale, and Ahab must confront it, risk his life: fold his life on the line by simultaneously confronting it. The subject—the fulcrum of the matrix that holds up the tissue of the world, on whose very presence the world as tissue is predicated, for whom the world is—vanishes. Its very place falls away. To paraphrase Freud on becoming subject ("Wo Es war, soll Ich werden"), in the place of the "tissue" where the "world" was, there come planes whereupon events, a-subjective individuations, come to pass: 5 o'clock, a wave, "a cloud of locusts carried by the wind at five in the evening."[73] To be, to exist (*être*) as a current of air, says Deleuze, is the highest [form] of life.[74]

iii.

In the viral register, inside the Zone, the tissue of the world is brutally, crudely (literally), undone—without spectacle, artifice, ecstasy, eroticism, imagination, subterranean cunning or dark passion. Once again, this undoing is not the destruction of the world as such. We cannot say with any certainty, as does Bataille during the war, "that of the world I was born into . . . soon there will be nothing left but a ruined memory."[75] Were this to happen, it would not be because of the virus. The world does not perish in the epidemic. It unmakes itself, incessantly deconstitutes itself, renders itself inoperative following two order-words that are the *dictats* of the virus: "keep apart" and "mask up."

The first order, "keep apart," prohibits intimacy (in every sense): touch, con-tact, contact with oneself (the face) and with an other; inter-course, intercourse with the air exhaled by an other, the touch of touch, of objects that have been touched. The prohibition dilates the interval, which is not nothing, not an opening to empty space; it "spaces," is productive of (other) spaces and of spacing: the elastic, rhythmic, flexible, spacing of bodies (motionless or in movement inside the body of a crowd itself moving, self-moving). The prohibition turns the gap, the condition of a relation, as we said, into an abyssal hiatus, which is "nothing"—a negation, a *néant*. It obliterates the in-between (the "inter-esse" that Arendt says is the proper translation of "interest"). Across the hiatus, a hole, an empty space in the world, nothing can pass. Not flirtatious desire, nor affection, or insult or a snub; not ardent passion or contempt or provocation, invitation, solidarity. Not even a helping hand. (Should you fall right in front of me, I would not be able to come to your aid by touching you.) Across this gaping hole where the tissue has been, every other mutates uniformly into any other: a body without a face, an obstacle in my path to avoid, as potholes are for cars.

The performative of the second order, "mask up," has been largely dealt with above: the surgical mask defaces. It does not hide or veil; insofar as it uniformly, by law, covers every face in public spaces, it is a barrier precisely to individuation, whose emblem is the paradoxically always unique *a* face.

The two order-words jointly undo the world or more precisely prevent it taking place in situ—in every place, in every instant, and in every instance where a potential encounter, a meeting of gazes, a face to face, a touch or a handshake or an embrace, does not / is prevented from taking place, and in its place, two atomized individuals—without recognition or encounter—traverse the same neutral, unproductive, empty space.

"What are poets for?" asks Heidegger, after Hölderlin's *Wozu Dichter in dürftiger Zeit?* (*Bread and Wine*). Why poets in destitute times? The question returns today regarding philosophy as what is philosophy for when the world is gone, when it absents itself? Or rather, what is philosophy to be, what could philosophy still be, when it is the word (philosophy's ground, terrain, *sol*) that destitutes itself?

"We cannot fall out of this world" is how Freud rationalizes, gives an "ideational content" to the vague "oceanic feeling" (untreatable by his science) that his friend Romain Rolland proposes in order to rescue something of the religious from the critique of *The Future of an Illusion*.[76] Nothing mystical, he says, but a common sentiment of a oneness, of having a binding bond so that one is never without (outside) the world, intuited as the whole or the cosmos.

(Today, of course, one wonders about the contemporaneity of

this sentiment, of how many of the millions still hold onto this notion, even as an illusion, as they are chased from their homes, hunted down in their own world, dying on the seas and in deserts, only to find their passage blocked to somewhere / anywhere by patrols, vigilantes, border and other walls of exclusion and / or confinement. Do they not have the immediate, unmediated experience of the facticity of having absolutely no place on the surface of the Earth? Against Kant's law of hospitality, which, as Derrida also taught us, demands that the limited surface of the sphere that the Earth is not be appropriated as property.)

Well before this latest test by the reality principle, Freud's new science will have shown the "subjective fact" his friend posits against the illusion of religion to be just that, an illusion of facticity, a remnant of the fully narcissistic ego, retained as the memory of fusion before the "world" would have become world—distinct, separate, the external source of displeasure and pain.

If this old *histoire* has any bearing on our discussion here it is because of the illusion the sentiment and its analytic critique silently share as their common ground; for what the oceanic feeling of unconditional inclusion in oneness and its analytic critique as compensation for its loss have in common is the non-thought, or the unthought thought that itself has turned out to be an illusion; namely, that the world—whether or not one can or cannot fall out of it—remains; that the Earth remains, remains to be there (da-sein) to inhabit (poetically or not), to establish one's home (*demeure*) in it, even or especially in "dark times" (Arendt). That no matter what misfortune, catastrophe, disaster—war, famine, genocide, civil war, pestilence, nuclear meltdown, or even natural disaster, tsunami, earthquake, volcanic explosion should destroy the world here and now—the Earth remains, as Freud "senses" the sentiment, "eternal," or in the language of Derrida, *indemne*, literally, non-damned. The Earth has never been in question (even the concentration camp

Or, Finding the World Again

was a "continent"). The inexorable vanishing of the ground from under our feet was not, could not be a question for Derrida. Neither destruction nor deconstruction, it is the unthinkable unthought, not just for Derrida. Perhaps more than justice, it is the undeconstructible of deconstruction.

Here and now—is this a pre-sentiment? or an already firmed up knowledge?—the illusion no longer holds. The convulsions of the world cannot be dissociated from the violent trembling of the Earth, whose tremors in turn translate into catastrophes that here and there lead to the collapse of worlds. An experience not unlike when an airplane caught in sudden turbulence violently jolts. As the ground itself moves, it exposes its underside—the unthought, repressed void.

At the end of this long excursion, the question that has opened it and provided the pretext for it returns to me, one more time differently. It asks not to where or how should I carry "You" (whoever this addressee may be), but should I carry you? Should I be the one to carry you? And should I carry you to "here and now," where the world, rather than absent, lost, or departing, actively de-constitutes itself, interrupts its own becoming world, empties itself of "world"? In short, un-worlds itself?

We are weaker, needier than we thought at the start. In this time of the geocide, of *effondrements*, the need regards us, not an other, whose words would have been gone, who needs to be saved, to survive, be granted a "survie," which Derrida says is more than a life. It is us who are in need—of someone to come. Not "a God," but perhaps, maybe, a "dark precursor," *puresrpungforth*, who would reach us from elsewhere. Not to carry us to an elsewhere, which we know is nowhere, and which as we also know is not anywhere else, but to teach us, show us how to learn to live here and now. How to survive our survival of this epidemic time (should this be the case), how to invent the livable life of this life, in this world that is inexorably losing its ground. How to live in the time that remains . . .

Can this figure be Derrida, who, albeit with great irony, confessed to have never learnt how to live, to have not not thought of death a single day in his life? Or Agamben's contemporary, who stares into the darkness of the night sky to glimpse at something blotted out by the glare of light? Who, like Paul, is strong enough to break the vertebra of time, to fold it against itself, even though time this time is already fractured, not by a figure or an act, but by the abyssal interval that has opened between historic space–time and the time of the geocide? Or will it be Deleuze rather, who gives us the figure of the "dark precursor," who himself crossed desert times and *lived* the chronic crises of existence?

Whoever, whatever this figure or agent may be, we know we will have to make it come. This time, the time that remains is not messianic time, the time of waiting. We will have to force it to come, command it, compel it to come . . .

In other words, we will have to invent it.

This long essay here has been a modest attempt in preparation toward such a task.

---

1   Paul Celan, *Grosse, Blühende Wölbung*, in *Atemwende*, Frankfurt am Main: Suhrkamp, 1967, 93.
2   The text appeared a year later under the borrowed title "Die Welt ist Fort" in volume one of *On Contemporaneity, after Agamben*. Written in the aftermath of Agamben's influential small book (*What is the Contemporary?*), the writing focuses almost exclusively on the "actuality" of the difficult obligation announced in the second half of Celan's verse: "I must carry you." Today, when the epidemic has acquired the onerous title of "pandemic" and when the world itself has become a question, it is the sense of the first pronouncement, "The world is gone," that insists on being recognized urgently as having much gravity. The present essay, which may be read as a postscript to the last book or a prologue to the next, yet to be written, is an attempt to respond to this new urgency.

Or, Finding the World Again

3   Jacques Derrida, *Béliers. Dialogue ininterrompu: entre deux infinis, le poème*, Paris: Galilée 2003.
4   Jacques Derrida, *Séminaire. La bête et le souverain, Vol. II (2002–2003)*, Paris: Galilée, 2010. Page numbers are cited in the text.
5   In a touching moment in the last seminar, which reminds us of Socrates' adieu in *Phaedo*, Derrida reassures his student-disciples that they could do the work without him, but then, in between parentheses, "permits himself" to return to the subject the following year (ibid., 391).
6   Ibid., "Neuvième séance, Le 12 mars 2003," 354–6.
7   Zsuzsa Baross, *On Contemporaneity, After Agamben: The Concept and Its Times*, Brighton: Sussex Academic Press, 2020.
8   There have been several others, most notably Gallimard's electronic publication, *Tracts de crise*. The 69 interventions during the period of confinement in France were published in paper form as *Tracts de crise. Un virus et des hommes, 18 mars / 11 mai 2020*, Collection Tracts, Gallimard, 2020. On the virtual platform Rencontres philosophiques de Monaco, Joseph Cohen launched his *Antivirus philosophiques*, a series of 18 contributions between 11.03 and 08.05.
9   For Alain Fleischer's account, see *Time Machine: Cinematic Temporalities (Exhibition Film)*, curated by Antonio Somaini with Eline Grignard and Marie Rebecchi, and with Antoine Prévost-Balga as Associate Curator. The exhibition, which opened on January 12, 2020 in the city of Parma, was closed on March 8, 2020, because of the national lockdown due to the pandemic. At https://vimeo.com/499133645.
10 In a letter read on France Inter, Monday, May 4, 2020: "Nous ne nous réveillerons pas, après le confinement, dans un nouveau monde; ce sera le même, en un peu pire."
11 Since I wrote this, several vaccines have been developed and deployed, without disposing of any of these questions. The virus continues to mutate. It outruns us in the race, taking the globe as its terrain.
12 Marguerite Duras, *La couleur des mots*. Interview with Dominique Noguez. A film by Jérôme Beaujour and Jean Mascolo, 1984.
13 "Nous sortons d'un grand moment de certitude"; "nous sortons peut-être même de l'ère de la certitude." *Coronavirus, une conversation mondiale: comment vivre dans un monde d'incertitude*. France Culture, August 28, 2020. At
https://www.franceculture.fr/emissions/le-temps-du-debat/coron-avirus-une-conversation-mondiale-comment-vivre-dans-un-monde-d'incertitude. This series on France Culture is yet another "platform" responding to the immediacy of the urgency for philosophy to be on

time, to not miss its rendez-vous with history this time: ("Depuis le début du confinement, l'équipe du Temps du débat a rassemblé sur le site de France Culture plus de soixante-dix textes d'écrivains, d'artistes ou d'intellectuels du monde entier qui nous ont donné leur regard sur la crise en cours. Cette saison, cette conversation continue chaque vendredi.")

14 "Nous sommes passifs par rapport au désastre." Maurice Blanchot, *L'Écriture du désastre*, Paris: Gallimard, 1980, 9. *The Writing of the Disaster*, Lincoln: University of Nebraska Press, 1986, 3. Anne Smock's translation altered.

15 Jean-Luc Nancy, untitled opening session of the seminar *Voir le temps venir*, under the direction of Jean-Christophe Bailly, Jeu de Paume, Paris, November 8, 2019.

16 Jacques Derrida, *Specters of Marx*, trans. Peggy Kamuf, New York: Routledge, 1994, 19.

17 "I fear it serves nothing," "Je crains qu'il ne serve à rien." Jean-Pierre Dupuy, "Si nous sommes la seule cause . . . ," Interview with Antoine Reversion, *Le Monde*, July 3, 2020. At https://www.lemonde.fr/idees/article/2020/07/03/jean-pierre-dupuy-si-nous-sommes-la-seule-cause-des-maux-qui-nous-frappent-alors-notre-responsabilié-devient-demesurée_6045012_3232.html.

18 See Gérard Bensoussan, *Antivirus philosophie* #6, March 29, and *Philosopher en temps d'épidémie* #14.

19 "Ce que la pandémie met au jour, nous demande à nous interroger sur tout cet ensemble de projets . . . à l'intérieur duquel nous découvrons la présence insistante de la mort . . . " Jean-Luc Nancy, "L'utile et l'inutile," Festival Aleph 2020, Conferencia de clausura, May 31, 2020. At https://www.youtube.com/watch?v=nFFZI4Z6FQ8.

20 Sigmund Freud, *Civilization and Its Discontents*, trans. James Strachey, New York: Norton & Co., 1989, 44.

21 Maurice Blanchot, "On a Change of Epoch (1960)," in *The Blanchot Reader*, ed. Michael Holland, Oxford: Blackwell, 1995. I am citing this abbreviated edition here as it includes the date in the title.

22 Ibid., 176–8.

23 Another distant relation is perhaps the shift in sports that Deleuze takes note of: in place of marshalling brute force against force, as with jumping, lifting, even running against gravity, the new sports—surfing, gliding, skateboarding, acrobatic and even traditional skiing—compose with existing forces—that of the wave, the current of air, the almost frictionless gravity of the snow-covered slope.

Or, Finding the World Again

24 Michel Houellebecq, "En un peu pire, réponses à quelques amis," France Inter, May 4, 2020. At https://www.franceinter.fr/emissions/lettres-d-interieur/lettres-d-interieur-04-mai-2020.
25 Jean-Luc Nancy, *La peau fragile du monde*, Paris: Galilée, 2020.
26 See my "Agamben, the Virus and the Biopolitical: A Riposte." Included in this volume.
27 Ibid.
28 Michel Foucault, "Right of Death and Power Over Life," in *The History of Sexuality, Vol. I: An Introduction*, trans. Robert Hurley, New York: Vintage Books, 1990.
29 Christian Salmon, *La tyrannie des bouffons, Sur le pouvoir grotesque*, Paris: Les liens qui libèrent, 2020. "On voit depuis 2016, et pendant la campagne qui l'a précédé, un homme multipliant les figures burlesques, transgressant par rapport aux rituels ou aux images qu'on attend d'un monde, en bousculant cet univers symbolique qui entoure les candidats au profit d'un agitateur." France Culture, Les Matins, October 15, 2020. Unlike their precursors (Foucault, lacking contemporary examples, cites Nero, Mussolini or Hitler), who take their role seriously and can be still parodied (by a Chaplin or a Brecht), the contemporary variety—Trump, Salvini, Johnson, Bolsonaro—deliberately play the role of the buffoon.
30 Alain Badiou, "La comédie est une pensée du présent," in *Le séminaire: images du temps présent, 2001–2004*, Paris: Fayard, 2004, 19.
31 This is not to say that language, thought, critical discourse, and even comedy, do not suffer the daily humiliation of impotence in face of the "banality of evil" and / or the evil of banality (the two have become indistinguishable), the impower to render inoperative, to crush (*écraser*) by ridicule (Brecht's method), the dominant discourse. But this humiliation remains without justice being rendered.
32 Walter Benjamin, "Critique of Violence," in *Reflections*, trans. Edmund Jephcott, New York: Schocken Books, 277–300.
33 Stengers and I both belong to this generation, share the same burden of responsibility, of complicity without remedy, which raises the question of right: by what right am I writing *this* text here? And not some other, which would not implicate me, call upon me as witness for the prosecution against me? In response, not to exonerate me but "pour mieux comprendre," I am citing here from the letter J.M.G. Le Clézio sent to Bernard Stiegler with regard to this very question. (Stiegler, we sadly know, committed suicide earlier this year. Perhaps—but we will never know—he could not bear [*tragen*] the weight of living toward the "coming barbarism."):

On the Absence of the World, One More Time

> Je vous remercie beaucoup de m'avoir invité à soutenir l'action de Greta Thunberg, et la vôtre, pour que les générations futures vivent dans un monde meilleur. Je suis né à une époque où cette préoccupation n'existait pratiquement pas. Particulièrement pour ceux de ma génération, nés pendant la deuxième guerre mondiale, la question qui se posait était plutôt d'ordre politique et social . . . Cela dit, non pour nous exonérer de nos responsabilités, ni pour nous atténuer nos erreurs, mais pour mieux comprendre le chemin parcouru depuis cette époque . . . Le mérite de Greta, et de tous ceux qui soutiennent son combat—rappelons-nous le sens du mot écologie, la science de la maison, puisque le monde après tout est notre seule maison—c'est de nous placer devant cette urgence, cette absolue nécessité: examiner nos valeurs maintenant, faire nos choix sans plus tarder, décider nous-mêmes de notre avenir et de celui de nos enfants. Cela s'appelle la vérité, tout le reste n'est qu'un vain discours, une chimère destructrice, une mascarade sans issue. (January 7, 2020)

See
https://blogs.mediapart.fr/amis-de-la-generation-thunberg/blog/070120/jmg-le-clezio-pour-que-les-generations-futures-vivent-dans-un-monde-meilleur

34 Isabelle Stengers, "Preface to the English Edition," *In Catastrophic Times: Resisting the Coming Barbarism*, trans. Andrew Goffey, Open Humanities Press, 2015, 3.

35 Anselm Kiefer situates his work, often literally, in "deep time": buries his massive canvases underground, in the earth, or leaves them outside exposed to the "elements" in box containers, at times for years in calendar time. He lets Earth-time do its fossilizing, pre-subjective work—predating the final touch of the artist but also of "art" and the "subject." Paint, canvas, and other perishable matters are thus transformed into fossils of the present— memories of the future, of a future that may not be for us, our species, which is one reason why they need to be considered as prototypes of art in the time that remains.

36 "Il faut hurler," cries out the agronomist René Dumont in the 1970s: "We are going straight to death." "Nous allons à l'effondrement total de notre planète." At
https://www.youtube.com/watch?v=-Vb8MrZQK7g.
Even Jean-Luc Nancy, who in 2016 (*Que faire?*) still insisted on the present being a mutation in historical time, admits by 2020 that we are exiting civilization, at least a certain civilization, without knowing what are we entering into. "Nous sommes vraiment dans un sortie de la

civilisation . . . une humanité court à sa perte, elle va à une fin . . . peut-être l'humanité a fait son temps, du moins une certaine humanité." Jean-Luc Nancy, "Un trop humain virus," interview with Antoine Mercie, December 10, 2020. At https://www.youtube.com/watch?v=FF71AxvwCHw.

37 Blanchot, "On a Change of Epoch," 179–80.

38 "Departed from historical space" may also mean that we cannot immediately appeal here to Derrida's "différance." The concept, which still pertains to historical space–time, cannot be transported (carried / *trägt*) to the present across the abyssal hiatus that separates us from it; it cannot be offered up against a final end, which, in accordance with its law of différance, cannot but defer itself without end. Outside historical space, in the time of the geocide, the ending without end must be thought otherwise than a finality that cannot catch up with itself. For the quick appeal that Nancy nonetheless makes to the concept, see his opening presentation, already cited, at Jeu de Paume, November 8, 2019. At https://vimeopro.com/jeudepaume/seminaire-jc-bailly-voir-le-temps-venir/video/374175940.

39 Bruno Latour, *Où suis-je? Leçons du confinement à l'usage des terrestres*, Paris: Éditions Découverte, 2021.

40 Bruno Latour, *Où atterrir?* Paris: Éditions Découverte, 2017.

41 George Bataille, *Guilty*, trans. Bruce Boon, Venice, CA: The Lapis Press, 1988, 26.

42 Maurice Blanchot, "Sur un changement d'époque: l'exigence du retour," in *Entretien infini,* Paris: Gallimard, 1971, 394. "On a Change of Epoch: The Exigence of Return," in *Infinite Conversation*, trans. Susan Hanson, Minnesota: University of Minnesota Press, 1993, 268, translation altered.

43 Jean-Luc Nancy and Jean Francois Bouthors, "Coronavirus: 'seule la démocratie peut nous permettre de nous accommoder collectivement de la non-maitrise de notre histoire,'" *Le Monde*, May 18, 2020.

44 Bataille, *Guilty*, 26.

45 Blanchot, "On a Change of Epoch," 268.

46 Michel Foucault, "Of Other Spaces," trans. Jay Miscowiec, *Diacritics*, 16:1, Spring 1986, 22–7.

47 "Premier regard sur le camp: c'est une autre planète," Alain Resnais, *Nuit et brouillard*, 1955. Text by Jean Cayrol.

48 Primo Levi, If *This is a Man?* (in other translations, *Survival in Auschwitz*), trans. Stuart Woolf, London: Orion Press, 1960, 24.

49 The formula, freely adopted from Saint Paul, is repeated throughout Godard's *Histoire(s) du cinéma* (1988–1998).
50 Anna Akhmatova, *Lot's Wife (Лотова жена)*, trans. Tony Brinkley. At http://www.cerisepress.com/01/02/lots-wife#english.
51 Gilles Deleuze, *Difference and Repetition*, trans. Paul Patton, New York: Columbia University Press, 1994, 77.
52 Levi, *If This is a Man?* 123–4.
53 "Today, at this very moment as I sit at a table, I myself am not convinced that these things really happened." Ibid., 120.
54 Günther Anders, *Journaux d'exil et du retour*, Lyon: Fage Editions, 2012, 114, my translation.
55 "'Where are you riding to, master?'" "I don't know," I said, "just away from here, just away from here. On and on away from here, only in this way can I reach my goal." "So you know your goal?" he asked. "Yes," I replied, "I've just told you: 'Away-from-here,' that is my goal." At https://atrulyenormousjourney.tumblr.com/post/49070165513/the-departure-franz-kafka-i-ordered-my-horse-to
56 Roland Barthes "The Face of Garbo," in *A Barthes Reader*, ed. Susan Sontag, New York: Hill and Wang, 1982, 82–4.
57 Marguerite Duras, *The Lover*, trans. Barbara Bray, New York: Harper & Row, 1986, 4–5.
58 Ibid.
59 Roger Caillois, "The Mask," trans. Jeffry Stucker, *The White Review*, March 2015. At https://www.thewhitereview.org/feature/the-mask.
60 To this "everything" I need to add a recent remark by Jean-Luc Nancy: to touch another living being is to touch life itself. "Touche-Touche," conference presentation, ICI, Berlin, March 24, 2021. At https://www.ici-berlin.org/events/jean-luc-nancy-intimacy.
61 Jacques Derrida, *Le toucher, Jean-Luc Nancy*, Paris: Galilee, 2000.
62 Zsuzsa Baross, "Noli Me Tangere: for Jacques Derrida," *Angelaki*, 6:2, 2001, 149–64.
63 Charles Baudelaire, "The Man of the Crowd," in *Selected Writings on Art & Artists*, trans. P.E. Charvet, Cambridge: Cambridge University Press, 1972, 397.
64 "The world and the people who inhabit it are not the same. The world lies between people, and [is] this in-between." Hannah Arendt, *Men in Dark Times*, New York: Harcourt Brace, 1993, 4.
65 The concept in Agamben's construction is itself a space in between: ambiguous, ambivalent, it falls between the private and the public realm

and thus belongs to the possible World that is erected by this decision / division as fundamental, that is, founding.
66 Michel Serres, *The Parasite*, trans. Lawrence R. Schehr, Minneapolis: University of Minnesota Press, 2007.
67 That the system has been adjusted to control the bodies (temperature, movement, network of contacts) of the entire population during the epidemic is not a confirmation of Agamben's argument regarding the states of emergencies elsewhere. The "state" in China is not an exception, but the law. For a survey of China's system of digital surveillance, see Gabriele de Seta, "Optical Governance: The Role of Machine Vision in China's Epidemic Response." *Stelka Mag*, 10.11, 2020. At www/stelkamag.com/en/article/optical-governance.
68 Georges Bataille, *Theory of Religion*, trans. Robert Hurley, New York: Zone Books, 1989.
69 As we know, Bataille planned to carry out the sacrifice of a volunteer subject in the woods outside Paris.
70 Bataille, *Guilty*, 18, 30.
71 Ibid., 14.
72 See especially Chapter 10, "1730: Becoming-Intense, Becoming Animal . . . " of Gilles Deleuze and Félix Guattari, *A Thousand Plateaus*, trans. Brian Massumi, Indianapolis: University of Minnesota Press, 1987.
73 Ibid., 262.
74 "Être comme un courant d'air, pour moi c'est la plus haute de la vie," *Séminaire sur Foucault: Pouvoir*, Cours Vincennes-St Denis, Cours du 03/06/1986. At https://www.webdeleuze.com/textes/289.
75 Bataille, *Guilty*, 55.
76 Freud, *Civilization and its Discontents*, 10–11.

Akhmatova, A. (1924). *Lot's Wife (Лотова жена)* (T. Brinkley Trans.). *Cerise Press*. http://www.cerisepress.com/01/02/lots-wife#english.
Anders, G. (2012). *Journaux d'exil et du retour*. Fage Editions.
Arendt, H. (1993). *Men in Dark Times*. Harcourt Brace.
Badiou, A. (2004). *Le séminaire: Images du temps présent, 2001–2004*. Fayard.
Baross, Z. (2019). *On Contemporaneity, after Agamben: The Concept and Its Times*. Sussex Academic Press.
Baross, Z. (2020). Agamben, the Virus and the Biopolitical: A Riposte. First published in the *European Journal of Psychoanalysis*. http://www.journal-psychoanalysis.eu/agamben-the-virus-and-the-biopolitical-a-riposte. Republished in 2021 in paper form in F. Castrillon and T. Marchevsky (Eds.), *Coronavirus, Psychoanalysis, and Philosophy*. Routledge. 2021.

Baross, Z. (2001). Noli Me Tangere: For Jacques Derrida. *Angelaki*, 6(2), 149–64.

Barthes, R. (1982). The Face of Garbo. In S. Sontag (Ed.), *A Barthes Reader*. Hill and Wang.

Bataille, G. (1988). *Guilty* (B. Boon Trans.). The Lapis Press.

Bataille, G. (1989). *Theory of Religion* (R. Hurley Trans.). Zone Books.

Baudelaire, C. (1972). The Man of the Crowd. In *Selected Writings on Art and Artists* (P.E. Charvet Trans.). Cambridge University Press.

Benjamin, W. (1986). Critique of Violence. In *Reflections* (E. Jephcott Trans.). Schocken Books.

Bensussan, G. (2020) *Antivirus philosophie* #6 and *Philosopher en temps d'épidémie* #14.

Blanchot, M. (1971). Sur un changement d'époque: L'exigence du retour. In *Entretien infini*. Gallimard.

Blanchot, M. (1980). *L'Écriture du désastre*. Gallimard.

Blanchot, M. (1986). *The Writing of the Disaster* (A. Smock Trans. [altered]). University of Nebraska Press.

Blanchot, M. (1993). On a Change of Epoch: The Exigence of Return. In *Infinite Conversation* (S. Hanson Trans.). University of Minnesota Press.

Blanchot, M. (1995). On a Change of Epoch (1960). In M. Holland (Ed.), *The Blanchot Reader*. Blackwell.

Celan, P. (1967). Grosse, blühende wölbung. In *Atemwende*. Suhrkamp.

Caillois, R. (2015). The Mask (J. Stucker Trans.). *The White Review*. https://www.thewhitereview.org/feature/the-mask.

Cohen, J. (2020). Antivirus philosphiques. *Rencontres Philosophiques de Monaco*. https://philomonaco.com/2020/11/27/les-recommandations-antivirus-des-philosophes/

de Seta, G. (2020). Optical Governance: The Role of Machine Vision in China's Epidemic Response. *Stelka Mag*, 10.11.20. www.stelkamag.com/en/article/optical-governance.

Deleuze, G. (1986). *Séminaire sur Foucault: Pouvoir*. Cours Vincennes-St Denis. https://www.webdeleuze.com/textes/289.

Deleuze, G. (1994). *Difference and Repetition* (P. Patton Trans.). Columbia University Press.

Deleuze, G., & Guattari, F. (1987). *A Thousand Plateaus* (B. Massumi Trans.). University of Minnesota Press.

Derrida, J. (1994). *Specters of Marx* (P. Kamuf Trans.). Routledge.

Derrida, J. (2000). *Le toucher, Jean-Luc Nancy*. Galilée.

Derrida, J. (2003). *Béliers. Le dialogue ininterrompu: Entre deux infinis, le poème*. Galilée.

Or, Finding the World Again

Derrida, J. (2010). *Séminaire. La bête et le souverain, Vol. II (2002–2003)*. Galilée.

Dupuy, J-P. (2020, July 3). Interview with Antoine Reversion. *Le Monde*. https://www.lemonde.fr/idees/article/2020/07/03/jean-pierre-dupuy-si-nous-sommes-la-seule-cause-des-maux-qui-nous-frappent-alors-notre-re sponsabilié-devient-demesurée_6045012_3232.html.

Duras, M. (1986). *The Lover* (B. Bray Trans.). Harper & Row.

Duras, M., & Noguez, D. (1984). *La couleur des mots*. A film by Jerome Beaujour and Jean Mascolo.

Fleischer, A. (2020). *Time Machine: Cinematic Temporalities (exhibition film)*. https://vimeo.com/499133645.

Foucault, M. (1986). Of Other Spaces (J. Miscowiec Trans.). *Diacritics, 16*(1), Spring, 22–7.

Foucault, M. (1990). Right of Death and Power Over Life. In *The History of Sexuality, vol. I: An Introduction* (R. Hurley Trans.). Vintage Books.

Freud, S. (1989). *Civilization and its Discontents* (James Strachey Trans.). Norton & Co.

Gallimard (2020). *Tracts de crise. Un virus et des hommes, 18 mars / 11 mai 2020*. Gallimard.

Godard, J-L. (Director) (1988–1998). *Histoires du Cinéma* [Film].

Houellebecq, M. (2020, May 4). Letter. https://www.franceinter.fr/emissions/lettres-d-interieur/lettres-d-interieur-04-mai-2020.

Latour, B. (2017). *Où atterrir?* Éditions Découverte.

Latour, B. (2021). *Où suis-je? Leçons du confinement à l'usage des terrestres*. Éditions Découverte.

Le Clézio, J.M.G. (2020, January 7). Letter. https://blogs.mediapart.fr/amis-de-la-generation-thunberg/blog/070120/jmg-le-clezio-pour-que-les-gen erations-futures-vivent-dans-un-monde-meilleur.

Levi, P. (1960). *If This is a Man?* (Stuart Woolf Trans.). Orion Press.

Nancy, J-L. (2019). Untitled opening session of the seminar *Voir le temps venir*, Jeu de Paume. https://vimeopro.com/jeudepaume/seminaire-jc-bailly-voir-le-temps-venir/video/374175940.

Nancy, J-L. (2020). L'utile et l'inutile. *Festival Aleph 2020, Conferencia de clausura*. https://www.youtube.com/watch?v=nFFZI4Z6FQ8.

Nancy, J-L. (2020a). *La peau fragile du monde*. Galilée.

Nancy, J-L. (2020b, August 28). *Coronavirus, une conversation mondiale: Comment vivre dans un monde d'incertitude*. France Culture. https://www.franceculture.fr/emissions/le-temps-du-debat/coronavirus-une-conversation-mondiale-comment-vivre-dans-un-monde-d'incertitude.

Nancy, J-L. (2020c). Un trop humain virus. Interview with Antoine Mercie. https://www.youtube.com/watch?v=FF71AxvwCHw.

Nancy, J-L. (2021) *Touche-touche,* conference presentation, ICI, Berlin. https://www.ici-berlin.org/events/jean-luc-nancy-intimacy

Nancy, J-L., & Bouthors, J.F. (2020, May 18). Coronavirus: seule la démocratie peut nous permettre de nous accommoder collectivement de la non-maitrise de notre histoire. *Le Monde.*

Resnais, A. (Director). (1955). *Nuit et Brouillard* [Film]. Text by Jean Cayrol.

Salmon, S. (2020). *La Tyrannie des bouffons, Sur le pouvoir grotesque.* Les liens qui libèrent.

Salmon, S. (2020a). Outrance du pouvoir, pouvoir à outrance avec Christian Salmon. France Culture. https://www.franceculture.fr/emissions/linvitee-des-matins/outrance-du-pouvoir-pouvoir-a-outrance-avec-christian-salmon.

Serres, M. (2007). *The Parasite* (L. R. Schehr Trans.). University of Minnesota Press.

Stengers, I. (2015). Preface to the English Edition. In *Catastrophic Times: Resisting the Coming Barbarism* (A. Goffey Trans.). Open Humanities Press.

Sur-vie

The return here to this "old" text of Derrida ("Survivre," 1976)[1] has been inspired (incited, provoked) by Jean-Luc Nancy's reading of a short excerpt (December 2, 2020) on the YouTube platform that Jérôme Lèbre continues to edit, with the still timely title: "Philosopher en temps d'épidémie."[2]

I

"Mais qui parle de vivre?"? "But who speaks of living?" Derrida asks, asks himself in the opening sentence to this long essay "Survivre"—impossible to translate, impossibly translated as "Living On." Then he adds—and the impossibility of translation continues—"sur vivre," cut into two words. A modification not a precision, he insists, despite the adverbial phrase "autrement dit" introducing the supplement: "in other words [who speaks on or about] living?" (75, *119*).

This opening with a double question, neither a repetition of the same nor two different questions, functions doubly as a "discourse operator," to adopt Barthes' terminology. On the one hand, it launches the writing trait on its path of breaching a passage from the common or vulgar (*vulgaris*) sense of *vivre* and *survivre* as (mere) living and surviving (*Überleben*)—toward the creation (as Deleuze would prefer us to say) of a new *concept*: *sur-vie* (*Fortleben*). In a jubilant language, of which we should not lose sight in the course of this re-reading, the writing will give this new, singular sense to "*sur*(vie)": *more* than a life ("plus qu'une vie"), *more* than a lifetime, *more* than that eternity of life of which men often speak: a resurrection *in* life, in the time of life ("une survie dans le temps de la vie")—jubilant, in excess of all living (124, *168*). At once "survivance" and "revenance," it exceeds at the same time living and dying, supplanting the one and the other by a *sur*ge and a *sus*pension. ("Le survivre déborde à la fois le vivre et le mourir, les suppléant l'un et l'autre d'un *sur*saut et d'un *sur*sis . . ." [emphases added, 114, *153*].)

This first operation takes place in the time (and temporality) of Derrida's writing with which its effects are contemporaneous. The second performative, on the other hand, in the time of this re-reading, is the posthumous after-effect of this same incipit in repetition. On another plane and in another order of time—simultaneously with, but without effacing the effect of the first—it brutally shows us, at once exhibits and exposes us to the distance that separates us today from Derrida. Not only from this question of Derrida "mais qui parle?" (when in this epidemic time we speak of little else than living and surviving, living *as* surviving); not only from this text of Derrida that would sur-pass surviving as [im]proper living (when nothing would appear more distant, more impossible—untimely, but in the weak sense—than discourse that would cultivate indifference, not to say show contempt for survival). The distance, *l'écart* (*qui nous écarte*), is also from the time of Derrida, from the world-time (for time is world, as he himself wrote some three decades ago in *Specters of Marx*) in which these words were first pronounced at a conference at Yale. The Yale of Paul de Man, before the "scandal" of Paul de Man: an order of time—of world, discourse, cares (*Zorgen*), affects and affections—for which the name, the corpus, the signature "Derrida" was (and today perhaps more than ever still is) a luminous meta-sign.

In truth, this separation is also biographical, "personal." The same fault line also separates us from ourselves. For this time, at least for some of us, was also our time, the world-time of possible futures we still thought we had in common with Derrida—for some time after these words were pronounced.

Sur-vie

The double-handed operation above by "the one hand" and "the other hand" will be recurring throughout this re-reading of Survivre," a text that itself operates in between: in gaps and intervals, and as we have just seen, in between the two faces of the writing. It is from the interior of such other spaces that it sur-passes the border line of the defining opposition (contradiction) between death and life. The concept of *sur-vie* is exemplary of such a liberating move. My reading here will rely on the "duplicity" (in every sense) of Derrida's writing as it attempts to destabilize (blur, "liquify," or make run like color runs) another line, or the same line differently this time. In the time of this epidemic, it targets for deconstruction the definition, the solidity, the immobile determination of the border between living and dying *on the interior* of living dying.

The first question—"mais qui?"—is purely rhetorical. It neither awaits, nor needs an answer. It is the narrator, the questioner (Derrida), who speaks of life. Not only in this text, "Survivre," but throughout the entire corpus, in works yet to be written and still to come at the time of this conference. In one form or another, by one pretext or another, Derrida will speak of nothing but *vivre* and *survivre*—until the very last question of his last seminar: who is capable of death? ("qui peut la mort?"[3]); until his last breath, commanding us who survive him to prefer always life and affirm survival ("Préférez toujours la vie et affirmez sans cesse la survie."[4]).

In the second, grammatically incomplete question, the fragment(ed) "sur vie" is itself a performative: it inserts a cut into the common orthography of the vocable, or, in Hannah Arendt's forceful idiom, "acts into" the sense it makes and how it makes sense. Untying the two semantic units, the incision, and in other places the hyphen, releases the "interminable mobility" of the

Sur-vie

plurality of sense that the contraction in "survie" paralyzes; it sets free the overdetermined indetermination that links "sur" to "vie": the excess, the more—but also the "on," "over," "above" and "about"—to life, forcing the relation to hesitate, to actively "undecide" between different senses, forms, and modes of sur-vival; between what Walter Benjamin gives us, and on whose ready-made distinction Derrida often relies, as *Überleben* and *Fortleben*.[5]

This initial and initiating mobility will invade the whole of the *text*. The *writing* (and we will need to maintain the distinction between the two as between the space and the work of the writing) avails itself of the productive effects of this indeterminacy: extends it, recovers it, multiplies it, makes it work in between the texts it gives itself the task to read together, and in between whose "borders," "bordures," "folds," "limits," "cadres," and "frames"—which it solicits, contests, and transgresses—it makes something other, of a third order appear. "Borderline events" as Derrida calls them. Events the writing sets free but cannot control or take charge of. They belong to neither side of the cut or sense and come to pass in an other space–time, in the register of the "sur" or the "more"—more than, other than what is being said or can be said (of *sur-vivre*, *sur-vivance* or *sur-vie*), either by Derrida's "Survivre" or by the writings it relies on as witnesses and material source.

It matters little in what direction our reading would be forcing the sense of "mais qui?"—a simple interrogative, or ironic, skeptical, even mocking (in the fashion of "who on earth would still speak of living as bare life, as the mere *Überleben* of life itself?")—we could not claim to appropriate the question as our own today. Nor could we claim the questioner as our contemporary, either in the common usage (of being of the same time), or in the philosophical sense of an untimely precursor. Our

Sur-vie

urgencies, anxieties, reference points, and even languages have become other than (stranger to) Derrida's.

On the one hand, the epidemic, which brutally imposes the question of survival, imposes survival as a question, or indeed, as the pressing and oppressive preoccupation of *Überleben*, has turned our discourses impatient, literal, pragmatic, un-poetic, non-metaphoric; one might say, thoughtless; that is, constrained, unfree, reactive. Arriving from the outside, perhaps even from an Outside, the constraint is *incontournable*: impossible to evade, limit, confine, or draw borders around from the outside. It has no, it leaves no, outside. Were we to ask, as does Agamben, how not to sacrifice a livable life that would merit the name for mere living—or in Derrida's borrowed language (from Blanchot)—for a life "maintaining itself in a state of pure supplement"—we would still remain captives inside its orbit.

On the other hand, on an entirely different, discontinuous plane, the question itself has mutated. Its subject has shifted, away from the *vie*, *sur vie*, or survival of the "subject"; it has surpassed the living of what we have been accustomed to refer to as the "subject." In our private and public conversations, debates, disputes, in the proper and on social media—but also in countless works that still ask what is happening to us, to the world, to our future today—we are still asking about the life / survival / living of our fellow humans, or, as many do, of the "economy," or, as some still do, of "culture." But more gravely and with much greater urgency, the question imposes itself with regard to life itself: life on / of the planet, of all the living on the planet; or rather, more precisely, the life (survival) of the Earth itself. For with regard to life, the Earth, as we have come to realize belatedly, is not another "planet." Not a passive receptor of life, a terrain habitable or even hospitable to life (as those looking to find it elsewhere, on some exoplanet, would have it); it is not a place where to land, "où se terrir" (which is Latour's question). The Earth is the "operator" (I borrow this concept

Sur-vie

from Deleuze and his geophilosophy) of the movements of becomings immanent to life itself.

We are still compelled to ask, just as before, without end, how to survive. How to survive this epidemic and this epidemic time (and the two questions are not of the same order: one may survive the one but still perish because of the other). But for the first time in the history of our species (and we are compelled by this same history to strictly consider ourselves—not as humanity, or the *Dasein* of Heidegger who alone can die—but as a species), and for the first time we may be certain of this being the first time, we are now forced to ask if the Earth will survive our survival, survive us saving what remains of life— bare life or barely a life.

It is not only that the question of *vie / sur vie* has mutated since the time of Derrida to become: What life merits to survive? What survival merits to be lived? . . . Today, in its modified, radicalized form, it also imposes itself differently, as an obligation, as duty (*devoir*). Survival, in the most literal sense possible, the survival of all things living, of the *vivant* itself, has become a responsibility. Assuming it (even at the cost of our own survival, perhaps?) may be the last chance, not to restore the privilege of our "apartheid" among the living, but to save the dignity of the species that we are.

Still, we need to recall that the fault line in question is not the invention of the epidemic. The interval separates us not just from the question and the text of "Survivre" but, as I would also risk saying, from the corpus Derrida, from the deconstructions that carry the signature and the mark "Derrida." It predates the epidemic, which accentuates, maybe even amplifies it, but does not produce it. The cut is structural, literally fundamental: the line cuts into the ground and will not spontaneously recede, be reduced, or repaired. We cannot be certain when, or even if the

Sur-vie

precision of "when" may apply in its case, but it certainly installed itself some time ago. It appeared well before this latest interruption in the linear continuity of chronology by this epidemic, a Zone of time, on whose interior time does not pass and which itself is not a passage of time. The abyssal hiatus in question is of a different order, opening not to a new beginning or to an end, but to an ending without end.

An event of such order, a mutation not of order but of orderliness itself, could not have not touched the foundation, the ground, the "terre" of deconstructions, especially of Derrida's. This is why—and not because of the virus—that we cannot find shelter today in the writing of Derrida; this is also why to *not* seek the safety of its protection is what deconstruction demands of us today. Its faithful betrayal (*"jurer avec"* in Derrida's language) calls for a wholly other task, it requires an entirely different order of work: "translation." In Derrida's re-construction (or translation) of Benjamin's concept of translation: a donation, the gift of a "sur-vie," giving an afterlife (more than a life) to deconstruction itself. (A formidable task and prohibiting responsibility which I cannot enter here and dare only touch upon elsewhere.[6])

Still, the massive dislocation of our lives and of our time by this still unending epidemic could not not leave its mark on the fault line, leave it unaffected, unmodified, untouched, in the same place. It cannot not constitute its forcing, not modify it, if not with regard to the "essential" question of living (so sweet for man, says Aristotle, that he requires no justification for it), then to the question of dying, following Heidegger's, perhaps also of Derrida's, axiomatic interrogative: "Who is capable of dying?" "Qui peut la mort?"

II

"Survivre," the text, takes place, positions itself in between two great works, themselves at a great distance in the history of literature: Shelley's *The Triomph of Life* and Blanchot's *Death Sentence;* a romantic poem and a *récit*, as says the French subtitle in its first edition, omitted in subsequent editions and by the English translation. "Survivre," the writing, coverts this distance of genre and history to its own writing space: in between the borders of these (and some other) texts, in between the two sides of their folds, of their titles in French (*Triumph de la vie* and *L'arrêt de mort*), it opens an *other* space and an *other* time that belong to neither side of the board, or the fold, not to the one or the other side of the "récit" that is not a "récit," says Derrida, cut by Blanchot into two unequal parts, nor to the side of the poem cut off, interrupted (unfinished) by death. In this other space–time, it puts to work the "interminable mobility" of the double sense of each of the two titles in French, each hesitating, never cutting a line between living and dying, actively undeciding in which direction (sense) the genitive should work, whether "l'arrêt" is to execute or to suspend the "sentence," whether the "triumph" is to be by or over life. The effect of this play—of whose writing? Blanchot's? or Derrida's? Their difference in "Survivre" becomes progressively imperceptible—is the arrival of the already mentioned border line events. One of which stands out as singular, even among those other extraordinary limitrophic occurrences that in the texts contest, solicit, destabilize the line (as Derrida elsewhere often showed us.) The singularity in question is not an event on the border, it is border line in another sense: it borders on (not) being an event at all. It "takes place without taking place" (138), which may explain why Derrida calls it "absolute," using the word in the etymological sense of *solus*, standing alone, in this case, unlocalizable in space, its passage in time imperceptible.

    In the remainder of this text, I will stay close to this singular exorbitant non-event falling or rather precipitating outside every orbit. I will limit my attention rather to three discreet occurrences—for the same reason I hesitate to call them "events"—that co-constitute it, or better yet, let it come to pass in between: an apparition, a decision, and a resurrection.

The apparition

Something terrible, of a "singular character," writes Blanchot, "un évènement absolu," says Derrida (*170*), arrives without arriving to present itself ("Cette chose effrayante est arrivée sans jamais se présenter" [*177*]). It falls or hesitates in between, without landing on either side of visibility / invisibility: the one, the dying to whom it arrives, never sees it; she does not apprehend (*apprend, prend*, take hold of or grasp) what has happened and that it has happened to her. The other, who should not have seen it, discovers it only in the regard, in the unseeing eyes reflecting "the most terrible look that a living being can receive" (125). Of this reflection the narrator cannot / must not speak; of this the *récit* will speak only by preserving its secret locked inside the crypt of the in-between of two instances of death; and of "this" Derrida will speak by recourse to a neuter, neither subject nor object: *La Chose*, all the while letting us believe that the Thing is Death. It is Death that hesitates in between: two instants, two senses of *l'arrêt*, its retardation and its execution.

The resurrection

It passes between two "instants," two scattering[s] of the pulse like sand, for as Derrida reminds us not to forget, "she" (who remains without a given name, whose name, while called, is not given by the narrator) was already dead. Having died already, she comes back to life in response to a call, in a living voice, "haute voix" ("I leaned over her, I called her aloud by her first name" [125]). This call is not the first, it comes in answer to a virtual summons by telephone right before it: "come," "venez." This second call is a performative in the strict linguistic sense of the term: it brings about the resurrection itself ("a sort of breath came out of her compressed mouth, a sigh . . . " [125]), instantaneously. It "accompanies rather than follows" her coming back to life. ("Cette réponse [*responsa*] épouse l'appel, l'accompagne plutôt qu'elle ne le suit" [*171*].) The passage is not to an after-life, to an eternity, outside, or as Žižek would prefer to say, with-out (both with and out, with but from the outside of) time, but to what is more than a life in the time of life: "Avant de mourir, dans ces 'quelques minutes,' elle a vécu 'plus qu'une vie'" (*168*). "Before dying, in those 'few minutes,' she lived 'more than a life'" (113, translation modified).

This *sur-vie* is a Yes! to life, its affirmation, indeed, a jubilant triumph of life, a triumph that is excessive, without limit ("I never saw her more alive" [113]). (Speaking of another resurrection, Blanchot's own, recorded, confessed in his *Instant of My Death*, Derrida uses an even more exalted language regarding this "triumph": "an ecstatic wrenching from the common temporal experience, an immense orgiastic jouissance" [*Demeure*, 68]). This *sur-vie*, which is "not to live or, not living, to maintain oneself, without life, in a state of pure supplement" (translation modified). (Here Derrida comes closest to a philosophical contempt for survival, by second hand, by citing Blanchot's word, and, by way of rejection, to anticipating the mere survival that will be at stake at the limit between living and dying in epidemic times.) Significantly, however, resurrected life has not done with death; it remains to be lived "with-out" death (again in Žižek's subverted sense of the adverb). A "sursis," it is lived at the edge, on leave from death.

The decision

"Vite, une piqûre" (*157*). Quick, a shot. The decision, taken quickly, is to die instantly. Not to commit suicide by the hand of another ("The liquid was slow to penetrate, but she saw what I was doing . . . Two or three minutes later her pulse became

Sur-vie

irregular" before it "scattered like sand" [113]), but, on the contrary, says Derrida, to assume the sentence, to take it upon oneself to be the executioner of "l'arrêt," in all the plural senses of this "sentence": to arrest (stop) death in its path of deciding, to take away from it the power to give death, the decision to decide the instant.

Such is then the scene, not of death, but of dying as co-staged in their inseparable embrace by Philosophy and Literature, which is not to say that it would be abstract, removed from life, or (mere) fiction. Today, in another world-time and an other order of time, we are the witnesses (and / or the survivors) of another scene, in another theatre, where dying is staged, its scenario scripted by the virus.

If, in speaking again (as Derrida cites Blanchot from another text), we alert ourselves to for long we did not speak anymore ("depuis longtemps nous ne parlions plus" [*153*]), this confrontation with the scene of dying as fictioned by literature, in another epoch, now past, brings something of the present to light, something that has escaped our regard, fixed as it is on survival, on the terrifying spectacle of the comatose body, face down on the hospital bed. It exposes—as if by a photographic *révélateur* passing over a negative—what the virus does, not to death, but to dying: the degradation, the debasement, the *bestialization* of dying in the sense that the French vocable "crever" reserves for the ending (*verenden* in Heidegger) of the animal, *la bête*. Moreover, this degradation and debasement will not translate to difference, differing, or even *différence*, no matter how heterogeneous it may be. It is not simply a dying in a different manner, more painful, agonizing, more terrifying. It is a ghostly deformation, a de-figuration of the scene of the fictioned theatre above, a trans-formation analogous to an anamorphic deformation, along trajectories starting from the same three critical reference points that determined the form / formation of the original: apparition, decision, and survival.

Apparitions

In the dark Zone of the coma, where no day breaks, the comatose is haunted by visitations—survivors tell us. Paralyzed, her body tied by the countless tubes and wires of life-machines to the hospital bed, she cannot shut her (already closed) eyes to the terrifying apparitions, cannot interrupt or wake from the procession of nightmares no dawn comes to dissipate.

Her solitude is absolute on the inside. She is alone dying and is alone with dying. No cry of hers—"come!" "venez!"—will reach the outside; no call (of her name) will break through to reach her on the inside. The last call—from an iPad or cell phone held up to her face—is for her to say goodbye before entering the Zone: a virtual yet absolutely real space (attesting to the reality of the virtual), or better yet, a universe of which she is to be the sole inhabitant.

A universe, once again, a space–time of indetermination: inside the Zone, life hesitates at every point between living and dying, between: a) turning the Zone into an abyssal interval in the continuum of life, between living at one end and survival to some more living (not to be confused with Derrida's "living on") on the other; or b) turning the Zone into the space where the continuum of dying comes to its end, at last. Either / or. In which direction the hesitation will pivot is undecidable, even by life itself. And if by hazard it is the "instant" that arrives last, the event of its arrival will fall outside of everything "human": presence, perception, experience . . . a fortiori, of testimony, of witnessing, even at second hand. That it was arriving, that its arrival was imminent, "instantaneous," imminently presenting itself . . . will not have been sensed, perceived, apprehended, grasped by the one to whom it was arriving. Life will have scattered like sand without anyone being present to it, without its

Sur-vie

passage having been lived or lived through in the proper sense.

"Survivors tell us": in other words, the apparitions and phantomatic visitations may be the fictions of survivors (or of my writing here). And yet, even then, or rather, especially then, they are powerful performatives: repair something irreparable, unbearable, insupportable; fill the void of the abyss, give it a content other than the "nothing," re-make the passage through it—no matter how terrifying, or rather especially as terrifying—accessible to experience. By running it through the mills of discourse, they re-present it as having been experienced, lived (as *Erlebnis*) or even lived through (as *Erfahrung*), travelled / journeyed through. In other words, even as, or especially if fictions—and not recuperations *a posteriori* of pure sensations that passed through and left their marks as memory traces on the body of the organism—they save dying from its bestialization, in Heidegger's sense of the simple ending (*Verendung*) that is proper to the animal.

Without such recuperation or reparation, one could ask if living dying on the inside would qualify as *a* life, whose immanence and a-personal force Deleuze celebrates in one of his last texts ("a wicked man," in a fiction of Dickens, lies dying in the deepest coma: "Between his life and his death, there is a moment that is only that of *a* life playing with death" ["Immanence," 28]). Inside the universe of the medically induced coma, life has been supplanted, its place taken by an assembly of life-machines that neither dance nor play. The Machine is programmed to combat, to win or lose to death.

The decision

But could it be still called a decision, when the moribund—gasping for her last breath of air, exhausted by the dying already done—consents to be "intubated"? Is this crisis still the "instance of the impossible decision" (115), or what makes decision in the proper sense of a "cut" impossible? There are only "calls" (of judgment) by a medical personage or team to induce and to end the coma. To terminate or let life continue. The request for consent comes too late, misses the critical instance. (As one imagines the form attached to the common, commonly brown, clip board is placed before her eyes, still showing above the oxygen mask cutting into the flesh of her chin. The fully gloved hand that holds it up extends from a body covered in a blue plastic cassock, the face both shielded and masked. There is no skin showing, no hand touching or "clenching" another, "pressing with all the affection, with all the tenderness" that it could, as Derrida cites the other scene in Blanchot [113].) When life's forces have already dissipated, when all that remains is bare life choking on the fluids of its own organ, "quick!" can only mean "more air!" The consent is not to live, to say "Yes!" to life, but to survive, to possibly not die, to not die now, if possible. (We may recall that Blanchot's fictional heroin also gives consent—to the treatment that may kill her. She too signs a paper, but to risk death "in an effort to live on" (137), to triumph over death, if only for a few minutes before dying. ("Il faut que d'une écriture signée, contresignée, elle s'abandonne et se donne la mort, qu'elle la risque pour tenter de survivre" [*180*].)

Survival

Neither *sur-vie* nor resurrection: the life that exits from the Zone cannot be anything other than the life that has entered it. Exiting at the other end, surviving the passage, could not be anything "more" than a bare life that barely survived.

Survival without resurrection, despite, not because of its intimacy with dying. Not the jubilant, "ecstatic," "orgiastic jouissance" which, as such, "en tant qu'elle," writes Derrida elsewhere apropos Blanchot's own *survivance* of the "instant," cannot arrive without being touched by, without having communed with death: "[il] ne va pas sans la mort" (*Demeure*, 88). (Perhaps it is also not without significance that when we speak of exit we inevitably invoke the name of the benevolent organization Exit that arranges death, its instant, by appointment: date, hour, place fixed by contract ahead of time, in the very same manner that one brings to an end [*verendet*] the life of domestic animals.)

But survival without *sur vie*: to what can it be an "exit"? What "more" can this "sur" signify? Nothing *more*, insofar as what is said to be hoped for a life *after* is "recovery" and "rehabilitation." The recovery of what has been lost: bare life or the bare-life functions of the organism and its organs (breathing, sleeping, mobility); its basic and most elementary senses (taste, smell, memory). While rehabilitation, or rather, rehabituation, is to habitus: habitual living, experiencing life in a "state of distraction" (as, Walter Benjamin says, we commonly experience architecture).

III

Blanchot writes in *Infinite Conversation*: "man is the indestructible that can be destroyed . . . and this means that there is no limit to the destruction of man" (135). The same holds for life, if we may assume that on Earth devastated, somewhere, in a crevice in the depths of the seas, a nano-form of life will survive our incessant destruction of life on Earth. Incessant, since we thought without thinking life to be immortal. The same (in)destructibility holds, not for death, but for the dying that must be lived / lived through. It holds not for death, not because death is "immortal," but because it itself is the end, the very last. It falls on death to bring to end, to "failure," the super-sovereignty of violence / *Walten* that, as Derrida says in his last seminar, reigns everywhere where there is living, as long as there is any living done.

For dying, however, for the dying that is proper to *Dasein* (to stay with Heidegger whose terminology Derrida also retains), the question of (in)destructibility—damage, ruination, degradation, bestialization—is more complicated. It is folded along several border lines. The categorical borders Heidegger cuts between different ends—*sterben*, the death only man is capable of (*qui peut la mort*), *verenden* (of the animal), and *ableben* (the medical / legal designation for the cessation of life only in man)—have been already contested from different directions. On the one hand, by medicine and all its technology and life-machines capable of extending life, that is, simulating life, ad infinitum in principle. (The figure of *coma dépassé* that Agamben also mobilizes in *Homo Sacer* names the limitless limitrophy of this animating spirit.) On the other hand, from the side of both common (sentimental) discourse and "posthuman" philosophy (embarrassed by the privilege it has granted to "man" throughout its history), the border line is destabilized, weakened, or even suppressed. For his part, Derrida heterogenizes, pluralizes these borders, complicates (folds) the lines of separation between the animal that cannot die and *Dasein* whose essence is to be capable of death. "Qui peut la mort," the one who is capable of dying is also incapable of *Veredung*, incapable of crossing the border to simple ending, according to the Heideggerian classification of ends.

The "bestialization" of dying, the notion and the phenomenon, or rather, the concept productive of the phenomenon, contests the same radical separation, stresses the boundary but from the other direction. Instead of undermining the separation in favor of the animal (see also Derrida's *L'animal donc que je suis*), bestialization weakens the boundary protecting the privilege, the territory, the life-domain of *Dasein*. It permits the "bestial" to contaminate it, to penetrate and corrupt the dying that is proper to man. Or better yet, it opens it to the permanent, constitutive danger of bestialization. At one end of the spectrum, there is the extreme figure of the *coma dépassé* (a dying whose unending falls outside of every sense and sensation, animal or vegetal); at the other end, the torment, moral

Sur-vie

humiliation and torture that mimic the pain and torment certain cultures, and in most cultures, children, inflict on animals. At the one end, the total abolition of everything that could merit the name "*a* life," and thereby of dying as *sterben*; at the other end, the unending incompletion of living that abolishes the dying that *Dasein* is capable of. Somewhere in between lie the infinite torments that, in the interest of survival, medicine's treatments are capable of inflicting on the sentient body that surrenders itself to them and must live through them,[7] "until death" (as says the judge at least in US courts announcing the sentence). (See Jean-Luc Nancy's account in *L'Intrus* of the aftermath of his heart transplant.)

"Qui peut la mort? À qui ce pouvoir est donné ou dénié?" asks Derrida penultimately in the last session of his very last seminar. In between the opening question of "Survivre," "Mais qui parle de vivre?," and these very last ones, "Who is capable of death? To whom is this power granted or denied?," a lifetime had passed. Yet, the abyssal hiatus in between remains immeasurable, unsurpassable. It is neither repeated nor replicated, only mimicked, by the unbridgeable distance that separates *sur-vie* from survival.

1   Derrida, "Survivre"/"Living On." Page numbers—from the French original in italic, the English translation in roman—are given between brackets in the text. When Blanchot is cited by Derrida, as is often the case, the page numbers correspond with the text of Derrida.
2   *Philosopher en temps d'épidémie* (#85): "'Survivre' par Derrida, lu par un autre," at
    https://www.youtube.com/watch?v=SUjIMxBy93M.
3   *La bête et le souverain*, Vol. II (2002–2003), 349.
4   Derrida's hand-written note read at his funeral. A photostatic copy closes the volume *Late Derrida*, ed. W.J.T. Mitchell, Chicago: University of Chicago Press, 2007, 244.

5   In his celebrated essay on translation "Die Aufgabe des Übersetzers," Benjamin, as noted by Caroline Disler, quickly abandons the conventional term *Überleben*, usually translated as the 'afterlife' of the poem in translation, for the rarely used *Fortleben*—living on or beyond. See Disler, "Benjamin's 'Afterlife': A Productive (?) Mistranslation In Memoriam Daniel Simeoni," at https://www.erudit.org/fr/revues/ttr/2011-v24-n1-ttr0381/1013259ar.
6   See my *On Contemporaneity, after Agamben: The Concept and its Times*, Sussex Academic Press, 2020.
7   See Jean-Luc Nancy's account in *L'Intrus* of the unending tribulations he / his body endured in aftermath of his heart transplant.

Agamben, G. (1998). *Homo Sacer*, trans. D. Heller-Roazen, Stanford: Stanford University Press.
Blanchot, M. (1993). *The Infinite Conversation*, trans. S. Hanson, Minneapolis: University of Minnesota Press.
Blanchot, M. (1999). *Death Sentence* , trans. L. Davis, New York: Station Hill Press.
Deleuze, G. (2001). "Immanence: A Life," *Pure Immanence: Essays in Life*, trans. A. Boyman, New York: Zone Books.
Derrida, J. (2010). *La bête et le souverain*, Vol. II (2002–2003), Paris: Galilée.
Derrida, J. (2006). *L'animal donc que je suis*, Paris: Galilée.
Derrida, J. (2000). *Demeure: Fiction and Testimony*, trans. E. Rottenberg, Stanford: Stanford University Press.
Derrida, J. (1998). *Demeure, Maurice Blanchot*, Paris: Galilée.
Derrida, J. (1993). *Aporias*, trans. T. Dutoit, Stanford: Stanford University Press.
Derrida, J. (1986/2003). "Survivre," *Parages*, Paris: Galilée. / "Living On," *Parages*, trans. J. Hulbert, Stanford: Stanford University Press.
Nancy, J.L. (2000). *L'Intrus*, Paris: Galilée.

JLN

Appendix

Here is my verse, not roses on your grave.
ANNA AKHMATOVA

For Jean-Luc Nancy, Posthumously
August 27, 2021

The last survivor died, just a few days ago. The last of the last great generation whose long line began almost a hundred years ago, with Lévi-Strauss, Marcel Mauss, continued with Bataille, Barthes, Benveniste, Lacan . . . He was also the last to write the eulogies, to speak the last words, if not over the body then over the corpus of his contemporaries. Of those closest to him, Derrida, Lacoue-Labarthe, Blanchot . . . but also Lyotard and Deleuze (who, with his long fingernails, as JLN wrote in his quasi-eulogy, folded contemporary thought into two heterogeneous domains, in which he did not recognize his own).

"And I live posthumously," he responded a long while ago to my book's title, *Posthumously, for Jacques Derrida*. "A terrible sentence," I replied. At once a cruel phrase and a difficult sentence (penalty) to bear: to outlive everyone, to be all alone, without living witnesses to a life lived, now in a hallucinatory virtual world of ghosts. A common pain and penalty meted out to those who live too long, outlive all the rest, are the sole survivors of a world in the whole world. "Each time, and each time singularly, each time irreplaceably, each time infinitely, death is nothing less than an end of the world," wrote Derrida, doing his own "work of mourning." Yet this world, absent, gone, "fort," as Celan writes, does not cease to haunt the survivor's world—each time just as unique, singular, irreplaceable—to evoke the apocalyptic visions in recent fictions and projections of the end of the world.

The philosopher's solitude, however, is not (only) of this ordinary kind. As Deleuze told us, also in one of his last texts—just before "L'Épuisé"—the condition of philosophy, for there

Appendix

to be philosophy, is a "society of friends." Not (necessarily) personal friends, although it is often the case, but a society with a taste for philosophy, for its "incorruptible discourse," as Derrida named, also late in life, the discourse that vigilantly watches over its own path, the paths it breaches, the turns it takes. If, today, nothing could be more lacking in this world than such a "society" with such a "taste"—as JLN observed not long ago, "sense makes no longer world"[1]—the end of the world of the last survivor, in more than one sense, is the end of worlds.

"And *I* live posthumously." I stress the personal pronoun in this cruel sentence: crisp, direct, factual, matter of fact; a statement, which, like any judgement (medical or juridical), is unequivocal, without appeal. (JLN's missives were always economic, at least in English [he persisted in writing in English]: no signature, no salutation, but ample punctuations—question marks, colons, hyphens—would give exactitude and precision to his missives, often claiming the last word.) He spoke of death with the same cruel facticity as of his own posthumous status and state. After the *Encounter*[2] with Claire Denis at the Médiathèque Duras—I do not remember how the subject came up (the theme was "le rapport sexuel" between his texts and Denis' cinema)—he spoke not of the death but of the dead body of Lacoue-Labarthe, his friend. In a few hours, he said, it changed, became something other. ("Life stopped traversing through it," I replied, alluding to Deleuze. This is also how I now think of his body, a "thing" in the world, emptied of agitations by thought, of age and disease.)

When I received the first missive, I understood "posthumously" to mean just as how I present it above: a survivor of friends, even if of friends whose lives have been co-implicated in and by philosophy. But today, just a few days after his death, and after I have just finished writing a response to the provocation of his reading an excerpt from Derrida's "Survivre"[3] (on Jérôme Lèbre's video channel)—which reading I took to be incongruous with the time of this epidemic, when to survive in the most concrete and brutal sense has become the order word, when survival in this same reductive sense is also our best, even final hope, for life on and of the planet—today, I see that there is, and there has always been, another sense hiding on the reverse side of this sentence and of the term "posthumous."

It is not that JLN's turn / return to this "old" text of Derrida (it was first pronounced at a conference at Yale on an unspecified date in 1977), that lending his living voice (only the voice, but not his "image") to the words of the dead—today, themselves posthumously celebrating a resurrection that is more than life in the time of life—was untimely in the weak sense of the term. Dissonant with the time *barely s*urviving what I call in the text (in this volume) the "bestialization" of dying, and not only by the virus. On the contrary, nothing could have been more appropriate, more timely *for the last survivor*; or rather, at once appropriate and inappropriate, at once jarring to the ear and yet illuminating. Except that illumination may not be, may no longer be the right word here. The image is withheld; it is left for the old raspy voice to transport the words of Derrida's "Survivre," to give them an after-life—precisely in this epidemic time—in the poetico-philosophical sense that these very words give to "sur-vie."

But for Jean-Luc Nancy, living posthumously also meant this: a jubilant life on leave from death (in fact, "endlessly resuscitated"). Having passed through death at least once already, his was a life lived in between (at least two) instants of death. It could not have been an accident that JLN was among the first, if not the very first, to take up in his seminar at Strasbourg Blanchot's late (last and only personal) confession: *L'Instant de ma mort* / *The Instant of My Death*. A text whose fictioned precursors, *Death Sentence* / *Pas au-delà* / *La folie du jour*, Derrida reads together (as he writes "one text reads another") for the first time in "Survivre." It is in this text (later to be followed by *La vie la mort* and *Des tours de Babel*) that Derrida first gives (donates) this new sense to *sur-vie*, turns it into a concept (in Deleuze's rigorous

Appendix

sense): productive of another possible life, a life resurrected in life. In Blanchot's *récit* as well, it falls between two instants and two instances of a "pulse scatter[ing] like sand."

In JLN's case, the first instance is the open-heart surgery of the transplant, in the course of which life in the body is suspended; the body becomes, as it were, heartless, the chest cavity having been emptied (he describes this in *L'Intrus* in great detail, leaving nothing to imagination).

Unlike the Covid survivor, who, when moribund, grasping for her last breath, only consents to be put on a ventilator and to enter the dark zone of coma without knowing whether she will die there, whether it is there that she would die, JLN decides. Without any guarantee (and against Agamben's advice: this detail, the precision of simply "Giorgio" as the author of the advice in *L'Intrus*, comes—one of Nancy's indiscretions—in a short riposte to Agamben's denegation of the epidemic as a health crisis), JLN chooses life. Unconditionally. Choosing it, even if he should die. Unlike the moribund who, in the IC unit, at the limit of her agonizing existence, is too exhausted by the dying already done to decide, Nancy consults, deliberates, and decides. Whether or not he knows (of) Derrida's "Survivre" at the time, he already chooses *sur-vie*: a life resurrected *in* life by way of a gift, a donation. A life given. It will be indelibly marked by this other decision (of an other) to give, to give a life, even if one suspended between two deaths, lived on a donated time with the heart of an other. A *sur-vie*, already in Derrida's sense. It comes before any writing on the body, before the volume *Corpus* (2000) and the corpus of innumerable writings on and about and around the body. Always already a jubilant celebration, it is a "yes" to life, a "yes" that is a precursor to / presages Derrida's last words, in his auto-eulogy: "always prefer life and affirm, without end, *la survie*." This life, in excess of all living, is not free of incessant torments visited upon and by the body, from the very first moment until the very end. Jubilation need not be confused with "good health."

Appendix

The last: in what sense is this *sur-vie* the last and Nancy the last survivor?—

On the reverse side of the narrative above, of this *histoire* of the last survivor, there is another figure, another concept of *sur-vie*. Inseparable from it, I would even risk saying, it authorizes it, authors it. This "last" is not the last one to live through or past a catastrophe, crisis, disease, or epidemic. It is the last philosopher who can speak without embarrassment of *sur-vie* (resurrection in life) *in* the time of this global catastrophe (the "geocide" of Michel Deguy), of which this epidemic, still on course as I write, is only a "novel" manifestation; when the mere survival of life in and of the planet is at stake; when time—out of joint, the time of *l'effondrement*—presents us, not with the obligation to carry the other, as in Celan's famous verse "ich muss dich tragen" (I must carry you). It imposes a new imperative, and one might say, the only one, or the last one; namely, to save the Earth when "Die Welt its fort," when the World is gone.

The corpus, the volume *Corpus* and the body of writings (whether writing the body or addressing the body [*soit à écrire au corps ou soit à écrire le corps*]), written over a period of almost 30 years, give a new, enriched sense as to what is more than life; in other words, give an after-life to Derrida's original *concept* of *sur-vie*, in the sense that translation (again, in Derrida's interpretation, transformative reading, or "translation" of Benjamin's text on the "Task of the Translator") gives an after life, something more than life to the original poem. The corpus and the *Corpus*, individually and collectively, set free, liberate, or actualize a plethora of possible bodies, each "plethein," full, overflowing with life: "corpus ego," "corps glorieux," "corps signifiant," "corps joui," "corps inspiré"; the sensible body of sense without sense (*sens sans sens*) that comes before and is the condition of the possibility of there being sense, signification, meaning, or sign; or again, the body, the hand-body whose imprint on the wall of the cave is at the origin of world / art /

Appendix

subject, all at once; or the skin-body, the body of *expeausition* . . . None of these is *the* body, none is finished, covered, contained, closed, enclosed. Life overflows the boundary of each. Space permits me to cite only fragments from a discussion with Jérôme Lèbre (*Signaux sensibles*):[4] examples of this overflow made manifest in a glorious language of jubilation (of life and of language, inseparably):

> Corps inspiré, oui, j'y insiste. Peau soufflée, insufflée, soulevée et portée en avant, au devant de contacts inédits, de touches colorées ou agitées, d'accents, de timbres [. . .]
> Pensez à ces quarante-cinq mille années pendant lesquelles ça n'a jamais cessé, cette sensualité spirituelle où s'éprouve qu'il y a du monde, des mondes, du faire-défaire-des-mondes . . . Comprenez comme ça se sent. Sentez comme ça se comprend . . . (69–70)

> La peau ne recouvre pas, elle forme, elle façonne, expose et anime cet ensemble incroyablement complexe, enchevêtré, labyrinthique qu'est l'ensemble des organes, muscles, vaisseaux, nerfs, os, liqueurs . . . ses ouvertures qui ne sont pas des 'entrées' ou des 'sorties,' encore moins des failles ou des fissures . . . la peau s'évase ou s'invagine, se retrousse et s'épanche ou s'exprime selon divers rapports avec le dehors. Les ouvertures ouvrent au-dehors, c'est-à-dire, le font entrer dedans ou ressortir dehors—nourriture, air, odeur, saveur . . . (65)

The question that remains to be asked—in what sense can one say today that this jubilation is / was the last *sur-vie to survive?*—translates to, or rather finds its answer in another. It regards the "place" (*lieu*) of this jubilation: does it (need to) silently assume—as its safe ground, *sol, terre*—the world, life, and the Earth *as indemne*, unscathed, undamned? As JLN himself wrote, already in *Corpus*: "Il n'y a pas d'existence sans lieu."[5]

Appendix

1. "Quand le sens ne fait plus monde." Entretien avec Jean-Luc Nancy, *Esprit* 3/4, 2014, 27–46.
2. Zsuzsa Baross (2015), *Encounters: Gérard Titus-Carmel, Jean-Luc Nancy, Claire Denis*, Sussex Academic Press.
3. The text "Survie," included in this volume, is a re-reading of Derrida's long essay in the time of the epidemic. Derrida's "Survivre" was first published in English translation in 1977 then in French, with the same title, in the collection *Parages* (1986/2003) by Galilée. JLN read a short but strategic excerpt on what is more than a life of life from this edition. *Philosopher en temps d'épidémie* (#85): "'Survivre' par Derrida, lu par un autre," at https://www.youtube.com/watch?v=SUjIMxBy93M.
4. Jean-Luc Nancy with Jérôme Lèbre (2017), *Signaux sensibles, entretient à propos des arts*, Bayard.
5. Jean-Luc Nancy (2000), *Corpus*, Métailié, 16.

Appendix

The Last Interview

I have already finished writing the essays in this book, even the posthumous supplement "For JLN," when serendipitously I chance upon what must be JLN's last public, recorded interview. Occasioned by the Prix Jacques Ellul in recognition of his life-time work, the interview took place sometime in July.[1] No exact date is given for the recording, but it could not have been long after, on August 23 to be precise, that JLN would die.

"Interview" may not be the right word. His interlocutor (Patrick Chastenet) tries to engage him, to keep him at least to the schedule of his prepared questions. But JLN is already in another space on the other side of the screen. His thoughts are elsewhere. ("We do not know where our dead (*nos morts*) are . . . Other cultures have always known it . . . I [individually] have always been always struck [*frappé*] by the presence of the dead in my life.")

It is a difficult recording to watch: the body cruelly marked by the proximity of death, the "subject" of the interview exhausted rather than tired by the dying already done. Not a self-exhibition put nakedly on view, but an unguarded exposure of (a) being vulnerable to the merciless recording of the digital apparatus and its archiving machine, without revision or editing. The discourse, which I can only paraphrase in translation, is halting, hesitating, at times lost in a labyrinth of its own making, in search of the right words, if not for something to say. It reminds me or rather resonates within me with the troubled letters Simon Hantaï sent to JLN[2] in the last year of his life: "'Je veux et je ne peux pas' (26.2.2008)"; "'néant' (27.2)"; "'rien' (28.2)." But there is only surface similitude within this resonance. SH's letters are often painful self-abnegations: "je ne sais plus," "c'est fini," "sans projet, sans attente," "bestialement nul," whereas JLN is unperturbed by his not-being-able-to-say ("comment dire?" "comment pourrait-on dire?"), even though this time, perhaps for the first time, it is not language itself that "stutters." The difficulty is not constitutive of what needs to be said, is not the only possible way of its saying.³

And yet, there are exceptional moments. Admissions, revisions, even amends are made for the very first time I believe on at least two occasions.

The first concerns the position of the "we"—JLN and what could be safely called the "society" of his philosophical friends—regarding Heidegger's "essence" of technology and the existential threat its infinite progress (mimicking the Kantian faith in human reason as the foundation of humanity and its constant, for Kant, moral progress) posed for the future of humanity: "we thought we could manage technology" ("Nous pensions que on allait s'arranger avec la technique"); until the very end, Derrida believed this to be the case ("restait dans une relative confiance à la possibilité d'avancer dans ce monde de technique"); we were always, for too long, progressist, "nous étions toujours dans une certaine idée du progrès," long after we turned away from political progressism; there was a blindness (*cécité*) at the heart of our thinking vis-à-vis technology . . .

He who, just a few years ago, in the strategically entitled *Que faire?*, still cited Althusser (humanity has always found a way out of its crises)—and who, as I should also mention, following his 2017 lecture in Budapest, dismissed my objection to his key concept of "mutation" in history as too weak to measure up to the unprecedented character of our time—makes an "amend honorable" in this last interview: today, we find ourselves in the remarkable situation, he says, that many who are now dead, like Derrida, like Lacoue-Labarthe, "I believe, would think differently today." (In my recent work, as well as in this volume, I ask about the precise sense of this "autrement": what does it mean for us today, if it cannot mean that we are to provide this other thought, thinking as it were in the place of those who are no longer present. It must mean something other than substitution or supplement, must mean that this work is to be invented.) "It is perfectly clear," Nancy continues, "that another recourse is

Appendix

necessary." There is either an alternative, or one continues with technology, to the possible end of humanity.

It is the surprisingly provocative question that immediately follows this last admission that lends it its unsettling force: "pourquoi pas?" Why not? Why not consider (think), next to the end (finitude) of individual life, the possible finitude (end) of humanity? For why should it continue? What opposes thinking the finitude of humanity in its entirety? These interrogatives are accompanied by another series of questions regarding the end (aim, length) of individual life, in particular Nancy's own: "I've always asked, is it better to live thirty years longer?" (the length of time he himself had been living with a transplanted heart). "No one can answer this question." In other words, at the end of his life, of having lived thirty years longer, and in a better position than anyone else could possibly be, he himself cannot answer this question. Cannot say, after the fact, an unequivocal "yes" to the life lived.

None of these reversals in the guise of rhetorical questions could have been expected to come from JLN, whom I've called here the "last survivor" in the last text I planned to close this volume, the last one to still speak without embarrassment of *sur-vie*, in the sense Derrida gave to this concept; who, more than any of his contemporaries, not only observed but in his work presaged Derrida's last words: "always prefer life." And yet, these questions—Why not? For what reason should humanity continue? Who can say that living longer is better than dying young?—are posed effortlessly, spontaneously, as if naturally or logically followed, or irresistibly flowed from the first set of dark concessions.

And yet, notwithstanding these exceptionally dark times, I must resist this "why not?" Without recourse to any "optimism," or saying "yes" to a future to come, or distancing myself in some other way from the "collapsologist" hypothesis, I am compelled to answer, as does a child: "because." Because it (humanity) *is*, like the spotted owl, the beluga whale, the yellow-beaked woodpecker (which some, the better among us, rush to save from extinction). This existence, "da-sein," being here, is not proper to us, it does not belong to us. Just like Kant's walk every afternoon at a certain hour, it makes a difference to the universe, it makes it differ from itself, however imperceptibly. In other words, the question "why not?" does not have an answer. It is properly unanswerable. The immanent, accidental, serendipitous, chance creation of inorganic and organic life, since the beginning of time, is without—falls outside the field of—justification.

1   Prix Jacques Ellul 2021: Jean-Luc Nancy, at https://www.youtube.com/watch?v=O5eZ9l8iHo0.
2   Simon Hantaï and Jean-Luc Nancy (2013), *Jamais le mot 'créateur'* . . . *(Correspondance 2000–2008)*, Galilée.
3   I always wondered about Nancy's justification for publishing these agonizing confessions of failure (to become like, Nancy, a philosopher, to write like a philosopher). I was especially unsettled as I knew Hantaï as the painter in the magnificent retrospective at the Centre Pompidou, I believe in the same year. I knew his confident voice, paid close attention to his very precise words (in a documentary shown during the exhibition) about his work, about his absence as a creator from the work: "let the (folded) canvas do the work." I even began to draft a text "In defence of Hantaï," in the spirit of Plato's lesson in *Protagoras*, on how to speak in the place of and in the absence of the one who cannot defend himself. I only abandoned my defence at the request of Zsuzsa Hantaï.

Appendix

JLN's Library (Fragment)

In private correspondence and in my writings, I have been citing, more and more frequently, Derrida's words of mourning: "Each time, and each time singularly, each time irreplaceably, each time infinitely, death is nothing less than an end of the world."[1] I would often refer to the always unsupportable "instant" as someone having been "sucked out of the world." Instantaneously, leaving nothing, not even a void in the proper sense behind. Nothing, not even silence, would come from the one whose absence is now only echoed by the emptiness of the banal, domestic spaces the "spirit" has vacated.

Then yesterday, in that curiously receptive state between sleep and being awake, receptive to semiconscious ideas often more real than the real, I thought about the three books JLN once told me were on the shelf of his library. Next to one another, I imagined, if classified by author, or, more likely, dispersed when placed in the chronological order of their reception. I could only imagine it, as I have never been to this library, that the three books were placed in a section reserved for the many volumes JLN must have received from countless others—authors, writers, artists, cinematographers—who were influenced by / attached to / admiring or only imitating his work. These books were not to be read, and almost certainly were never read, for as everyone understood, they were symbolic gestures, greetings, in homage, recognition, gratitude . . .

What will or what has already happened to my three books, I have asked myself still in that peculiar state. Were they destined to be discarded with all the other unsolicited gifts? Shredded to be recycled? The thought that they might be reincarnated as the pages of future writings in other books still does not disturb me. On the contrary, there is something pleasing about this immortality.

And what will or what has already happened to those few books that, as Derrida said of his own select few in his library,

JLN also "read well"? Read them without end, reading them to ruins, until their annotated, marked, stained pages were falling out. And what future is there or was there planned for the Library itself? Not a collection of books. Unlike Benjamin, JLN was not a collector. More likely countless assemblies, distant constellations of bodies of works (of philosophy and poetry, on cinema and painting [in the grotto], drawing and dance) that, possibly for the first time in their history, were brought to together, in the writing read together, and whose encounters, staged (forced, solicited, imposed, or invented) by the writing, gave birth to something absolutely new. A corpus of proliferating, irreducibly heterogeneous, infinitely sensible / sensuous bodies, for example.

Agencement: reading together. As Derrida said, one book reads another, but they read differently and not at the same time and not the same texts. (Uncannily, JLN's numerous video recordings continue to offer a sliver of a glimpse of the physical space, the library that was: a large graphic work in color on the wall, what looks like a drafting table with sheets, perhaps galleys in the course of being corrected neatly spread out, a section of a solid wall of books, almost uniformly white [Galilée?]). Will these books be abandoned? Or scattered? Executing Benjamin's unpacking of his library in reverse?[2] The other writer's exuberant account only intimates the destruction in edifice to take place: something immaterial, singular, never before and again in the universe will be "sucked out of the world." Or will the library be preserved (mummified), turned into an Archive? A sarcophagus or a sort of pyramid in reverse designed to not let the spirit escape? Not unlike the Warburg Archive, so carefully studied, among others by Didi-Huberman. But the relation of the library to the spirit is exactly the inverse. The spirit (anima) is the "animator" / "animateur" of a Library, which is not a world, but a universe in the cosmological sense; the incubator of possible worlds, even galaxies—uniquely, singularly and only in response to the

Appendix

solicitations, incitation, forcing of the "librarian." *Corpus* is such a galaxy, of body-worlds.

This production of worlds, of galaxies has now stopped. Still, the expression I cited at the top, "sucked out of the world" has been misleading, inaccurate. On his side of life, the ending is a torturous and painful path, painfully torturous. The destruction or dismantling of the world (as we are just discovering it on an entirely different scale) takes time. It must be lived, lived through in the sense of an *Erfahrung*. It takes a journey; it is a passage.

1. Jacques Derrida (2005), "Rams: Uninterrupted Dialogue—Between Two Infinities, the Poem," *Sovereignties in Question*, Fordham, 140.
2. At https://vimeo.com/374175940.
3. Walter Benjamin (1969), "Unpacking My Library," *Illuminations*, trans. Harry Zohn, Schocken Books, 1969.

www.ingramcontent.com/pod-product-compliance
Lightning Source LLC
Chambersburg PA
CBHW071413300426
44114CB00016B/2282